3/02

641.64
Pivonka, Elizabeth.
Five a day : the better
health cookbook : savor the
flavor of fruits and
vegetables
Emmaus, Penn. : Rodale,
2002.

JUL 3 1 2002

md. 5/16/11 mw

.02   03   09
7/11   11/   1

ILL JUN 02

GAYLORD MG

6/02

5 a day

the better
health cookbook

5 a day

the better health cookbook

savor the flavor of fruits and vegetables

dr. elizabeth pivonka
and barbara berry

Produce for Better Health Foundation

Produced by The Philip Lief Group, Inc.

RODALE

Notice

This book is intended as a reference volume only, not as a medical manual. The information given here is designed to help you make informed decisions about your health. It is not intended as a substitute for any treatment that may have been prescribed by your doctor. If you suspect that you have a medical problem, we urge you to seek competent medical help.

Printed in the United States of America
Rodale Inc. makes every effort to use acid-free ∞, recycled paper ♻.

Cover and Interior Designer: Tara Long
Front Cover Photographer: Mitch Mandel/Rodale Images

Library of Congress Cataloging-in-Publication Data

Pivonka, Elizabeth.
    Five a day : the better health cookbook : savor the flavor of fruits and
    vegetables / by Elizabeth Pivonka, Barbara Berry.
        p.   cm.
    ISBN 1–57954–528–9 hardcover
    1. Cookery (Fruit) 2. Cookery (Vegetables) 3. Menus. I. Berry,
  Barbara. II. Title.
  TX811 .P49 2002
  641.6'4—dc21   2001004512

Distributed to the book trade by St. Martin's Press

2 4 6 8 10 9 7 5 3 1   hardcover

Visit us on the Web at www.rodalestore.com, or call us toll-free at (800) 848-4735.

WE **INSPIRE** AND **ENABLE** PEOPLE TO IMPROVE
THEIR LIVES AND THE WORLD AROUND THEM

contents

5 a day: the better health plan

Imagine a scientific discovery that could save 3 to 4 million people a year from developing cancer; that would reduce your risk of heart disease by 40 percent; that could knock out almost half of neural birth defects; that may help eliminate the need for high blood pressure medication, and help control blood sugar naturally. This one amazing development could save us billions of dollars a year in medical costs, lost productivity, and lost lives.

And if this one discovery were available, who wouldn't jump at the chance to get their hands on it?

Here's the good news: This health-protecting marvel has already been discovered, and it's just sitting in your supermarket waiting for you. Walk down the produce aisle, stroll through the frozen food section, and take a look at the endless rows of canned goods. That's right—this wonder-discovery is (are you ready?) plain old fruits and vegetables. Eating 5 or more servings of produce a day will help you reap a host of health benefits—and much, much more.

The fruits and vegetables that fill our supermarkets and farm markets are overflowing with health-protecting nutrients. They're full of vitamins and minerals that keep your body strong and ward off illness and disease. They're packed with antioxidants, chemicals that protect you from free radicals—substances in your body that go around causing the cell damage that may

 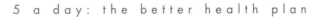

cause cancer, heart disease, cataracts, and other health problems. They also contain phytonutrients, natural plant supplements that work with vitamins, minerals, and fiber to protect against disease. Add all this to the fact that fruits and vegetables are one of the top sources of dietary fiber—which can do everything from helping lower your cholesterol and control your blood sugar to preventing gastrointestinal problems and helping you lose weight—and you'll realize that no other food or supplement can even touch the prevention and healing power of fruits and vegetables.

If that's not enough, consider some other reasons to strive to get more fruits and vegetables in your daily diet:

It's easy. Eat 5 or more servings a day—that's it. Nothing more to it. (And a serving size is smaller than you think! Check out "What Is a Serving?" on page 14.) No hidden costs, agendas, commitments, or number crunching, and there's no fine print to read. It couldn't get any more basic or simple. Yet, from this one easy change in your lifestyle, you'll receive endless benefits, from having more energy to gaining a top defense against a host of diseases.

It's fun. Eating 5 or more servings a day gets you to try new foods, experiment with new cooking styles and techniques, and cook up new recipes. You'll open yourself up to a whole new world of colors, textures, tastes, and smells. There's no hard work here, just having fun choosing, preparing, and eating all the fruits and vegetables you like.

It's delicious. What better way to protect your health than by tasting some of the best food nature has to offer? Whether you enjoy each fruit or vegetable in its natural goodness or use them as part of mouthwatering recipes, you can't find a tastier way to protect your well-being.

It's inexpensive. While some may say that fruits and vegetables are a bit pricey, compare them with the cost of supplements, medications, and medical bills. It's possibly the cheapest form of proven health protection out there. When you measure up the health benefits you get from eating 5 or more servings a day, the worth of produce is immeasurable.

With the Produce for Better Health Foundation's *5 A Day: The Better Health Cookbook*, eating 5 or more servings a day is even more fun, more delicious, more inexpensive, and easier than ever! It's packed with more than 150 recipes that have received the Produce for Better Health 5 A Day Stamp of Approval. That means each recipe has at least 1 serving of a fruit or vegetable, and is low in fat, cholesterol, and sodium—helping you reach the all-important health goal of 5 or more servings a day.

The History of 5 A Day

This cookbook is part of the 5 A Day for Better Health program—an initiative to increase consumer awareness of the importance of eating fruits and vegetables and to provide information on how to turn these recommendations into dietary practices. The 5 A Day program, cosponsored by the Produce for Better Health Foundation and the National Cancer Institute (NCI), is the nation's largest public/private partnership and the largest-ever nutrition education initiative. The program's goal is to get all Americans to eat a *minimum* of 5 servings each day to decrease disease risk. Reaching that goal could have a massive impact on protecting your and your family's health.

The Substitution Solution

By using fruits and vegetables in place of typical ingredients in some foods, you'll not only reach your 5 A Day goal faster but you'll often cut out fat and calories, too. Try some of these in place of traditional ingredients:

Use	Instead of
½ cup applesauce, for baking	½ cup oil
½ cup unsweetened pineapple, apple, or orange juice, for salad dressing	½ cup oil
½ cup baby food prunes, for baking	½ cup butter or margarine
Dried fruit, for muffins and quick breads	Nuts
Beans and chopped vegetables, for casseroles, stir-fries, and chilies	Half the meat in the recipe
Portobello mushroom, for burgers	Ground beef
Mashed potatoes, for savory pie or quiche crusts	Flaky crusts

The Produce for Better Health Foundation is an educational nonprofit association that seeks to improve the health of all Americans through increased produce comsumption partnerships among the health community, government agencies, the fruit and vegetable industry, and the private sector.

The 5 A Day wave started in California in 1988. Research was mounting, explaining how eating more fruits and vegetables could protect people from an entire list of health problems. Knowing that residents weren't eating enough produce—estimates were around only 2.5 servings a day—the State of California Department of Health Services with a grant from NCI developed the California 5 A Day program to educate people about the need to eat 5 or more servings a day.

Why 5? Based on the scientific literature, experts determined that 5 servings was the minimum needed to provide the full range of health benefits and to get adequate amounts of important nutrients such as folic acid. If people could strive for 5, they in effect would practically double fruit and vegetable consumption.

Just as important, the experts chose 5 because it was a reasonable number, easily attainable for the average person, and therefore, it was more likely that people would be successful.

California's initiative proved so successful that it was decided to bring the 5 A Day message to the entire nation. So in 1991, the Produce for Better Health Foundation was formed with the intent to educate people about the health benefits of eating fruits and vegetables. Working with the NCI and the original California program, the Foundation created the national 5 A Day for Better Health program.

Today, more than 1,800 organizations promote the 5 A Day campaign, including the Centers for Disease Control, the American Cancer Society, the American Heart Association, the U.S. Department of Agriculture, the American Dietetic Association, and the National Alliance for Nutrition and Activity. The foundation also works with health officials on the importance of placing fruits and vegetables first in the nation's nutrition policies.

5 A Day Quick Tip

To learn more about fruits and vegetables and such—including selection, storage, nutritional information, and a recipe of the week, visit www.aboutproduce.com, a Web site created by the Produce for Better Health Foundation and Produce Marketing Association. Also visit the Produce for Better Health Foundation's Web site, www.5aday.com, for delicious, easy to make recipes, the latest news on produce, and educational activities for children

Over the past decade, the 5 A Day message has expanded into the U.S. Uniformed Services, school classrooms and cafeterias across the nation; the nutrition education of the Women, Infants, and Children Program; the Farmer's Market Nutrition Program; and the Child and Adult Care Food Program.

The 5 A Day message has been a successful one: According to the Office of Disease Prevention and Health Promotion, 35 percent of Americans meet or exceed the goal of eating 5 or more fruits and vegetables a day. The USDA also found that the average American eats 4.4 servings a day—an increase of half a serving from 3.9 when the program started in 1991. To show you how such a little change means a lot, research estimates that a ½ serving increase could reduce cancer rates nationwide by 7 percent.

What 5 A Day Can Do for You

Whatever health condition you want to fight off, chances are that fruits and vegetables can help you win your battle. They put up a great defense against serious diseases such as heart disease and cancer, and they've also been found to stave off or at least delay chronic health problems.

Although modern science has discovered a lot of impressive health advances, nothing even comes close to generating produce's proven results. Studies have found that supplements containing nutrients often don't come close to achieving the benefits of eating the real thing.

Here's a sampling of the latest research on what eating a minimum of 5 fruits and vegetables a day can do for you.

Heart Disease

Coronary heart disease is the number one cause of death in the United States, and is the most common and most serious form of cardiovascular disease. Current evidence suggests that fruits and vegetables play a strong protective role in the fight against coronary heart disease. In fact, research estimates that by eating more fruits and vegetables, we could reduce heart disease risk by 20 to 40 percent.

Experts believe that fruits and vegetables provide protection in several ways. First, antioxidants such as vitamin C (in citrus fruits), beta-carotene and other carotenoids (in yellow-colored fruits and vegetables such as squashes, carrots, and peaches), and flavonoids (in onions) may reduce the risk of heart disease by blocking the oxidation of cholesterol in the arteries. It's that oxidation of cholesterol that causes hardening of the arteries and heart disease. Also, researchers believe that the B vitamins folate, B_6, and B_{12} help lower levels of homocysteine, an amino acid in your blood that is a known risk factor for heart disease. Finally, fruits and vegetables are rich in soluble fiber, which has been shown to control cholesterol levels.

Cancer

Cancer is the second-leading cause of death, with 1.3 million new cases diagnosed in this country each year. A diet rich in fruits and vegetables, combined with regular exercise, can reduce cancer rates as much as 30 to 40 percent. This translates globally to approximately 3 to 4 million cases a year that could be prevented. It's been estimated that 30 to possibly even 70 percent of all cancer deaths are diet-related. Researchers believe that fruits and vegetables contain many cancer-blocking substances, including more than 100 beneficial vitamins, minerals, phytonutrients, and fiber.

Stroke

Stroke is the third-leading cause of death and kills about 160,000 of the 500,000 Americans who have a stroke each year. Fruits and vegetables help control high blood pressure and reduce the risk of blood clots, two factors that can lead to a stroke. People who eat more fruits and vegetables may be able to decrease their risk of stroke by as much as 25 percent. The mineral potassium—found in many fruits and vegetables—may be responsible for the stroke protection, although some researchers also think that flavonoids found in produce help prevent both stroke and heart disease.

High Blood Pressure

About one-quarter of American adults—43 million people—have high blood pressure, which can cause heart disease, heart attacks, and strokes.

What Fruits and Vegetables Can Do for You

Choosing a variety of fruits and vegetables every day will do more than keep you from getting bored; it will help protect you from a whole host of diseases. Each fruit and vegetable family has its own unique disease-proofing and health-protecting properties. By making sure that you regularly eat from each category, you're giving yourself the widest health protection possible.

Citrus fruits: Phytonutrients in oranges, tangerines, and grapefruit may help the body resist cancer-causing chemicals called carcinogens, prevent harmful blood clotting, and avoid blindness.

Melons, berries: Melons and berries of all kinds may boost the immune system and help lower cholesterol levels. This family also includes kiwifruit, cucumbers, squash, and pumpkins.

Grapes: Red, Concord, and other deeply pigmented grapes especially may help fight against cancer-causing chemicals, protect DNA in cells, and prevent harmful blood clots that trigger heart attacks and strokes.

Cabbage family: Broccoli, cauliflower, Brussels sprouts, kale, bok choy, collards, turnips, mustard greens, kohlrabi, and watercress may lower the risk of hormone-related cancers, help protect DNA, and boost the body's ability to fight off cancer.

Deep-yellow and orange fruits and vegetables and leafy greens: Phytonutrients in apricots, persimmons, cantaloupe, sweet potatoes, pumpkins, and carrots may help protect against cancer, the buildup of fatty plaque in the arteries, blood clots, and loss of eyesight. Spinach, kale, and dark leafy greens have similar health benefits.

Tomatoes, eggplant: Tomatoes and eggplant may prevent carcinogens from forming, shield cells from cancer-causing chemicals, and neutralize cancer-causing free radicals. Tomato products such as ketchup, tomato sauce, and salsa may reduce prostate cancer and heart attack risk.

Onions, garlic, leeks, chives: This class of vegetables may help the body produce less cholesterol, block cancer-causing chemicals, control cancer cells, and eliminate other toxic chemicals that enter your body.

Other fruits and vegetables: Vegetables such as artichokes and stone fruits including peaches, plums, nectarines, and cherries—as well as pears, apples, mangoes, bananas, and avocados—provide fiber, folate, potassium, and other nutrients that reduce the risk of heart disease and cancer. The mono-unsaturated fat, vitamin E, and phytonutrients in avocados help protect against heart disease, some cancers, and macular degeneration.

Fresh, frozen, canned, dried, juiced: Frozen fruits and vegetables contain nutrients similar to freshly harvested produce. Other processed fruits and vegetables retain most of their nutrient, fiber, and phytochemical value. Steaming and microwaving help maintain the vitamin C and folate content of vegetables.

Soybeans, tofu, soy milk, dried beans: Phytochemicals in soybeans may block hormone-related cancers, stimulate the immune system, and slow tumor growth, especially in the colon. Beans that contain fiber, iron, protein, and folate—a B vitamin that builds blood cells—help prevent neural tube defects, and may help prevent heart attacks.

Diets rich in fruits and vegetables have been shown to reduce blood pressure levels both in people with and without hypertension. With the right diet and lifestyle changes, some people are even able to go off their blood pressure medication. (Never stop taking any medication without your doctor's approval.)

Diabetes

About 2,200 people are diagnosed with diabetes each day. Fruits and vegetables help keep blood sugar levels down and control diabetes. The fiber in produce has a protective effect on the cholesterol levels in people with diabetes. Fruit and vegetable intake can also help prevent obesity, which is a major risk factor for developing Type 2 diabetes.

Cataracts

Studies have found that people who eat more fruits and vegetables have five times less risk of developing cataracts, the number one cause of blindness in the world. Cataracts form when oxidation causes damage to protein in the eye, rendering the lens unable to function. Antioxidants such as vitamin C and carotenoids, found widely in fruits and vegetables, are recognized as the best line of defense against the oxidation that causes cataracts. The risk of cataracts increases from 5 percent at age 65 to 40 percent for those 75 and older. In the United States, age-related cataracts cost $5 billion a year—the largest single item in Medicare expenditures.

Diverticulosis

This condition has been called the by-product of Americans' affinity for refined and processed food.. Approximately one-third of Americans over age 50 develop diverticulosis, a condition where small pouches develop in the large intestine or colon. When the pouches become inflamed, people experience abdominal pain, fever, and tenderness. High-fiber foods provide the best defense against the development of diverticulosis. The best sources of fiber in the diet comes from fruits, vegetables, and whole grains.

Osteoporosis

About one out of every five women can expect to develop osteoporosis, a weakening of the bones that can lead to fractures, in her lifetime. A study at Tufts University in Medford, Massachusetts, suggests that alkaline-producing foods and nutrients such as potassium and magnesium found in fruits and vegetables play a part in protecting bone mineral density. Combined with weight-bearing exercise and adequate calcium, fruits and vegetables may help protect against the development of osteoporosis.

Birth Defects

About 3 to 4 weeks after an egg is fertilized, the neural tube, which eventually becomes the spinal tube, begins to close. But in some cases, the tube never or imperfectly closes, and the child develops spina bifida, often resulting in hydrocephalus and other neurological disorders. In the United States, about 2,500 infants are born each year with this condition. It's been proven that if women consume 400 micrograms of the B vitamin folic acid daily before conception and during pregnancy, half of all neural tube birth defects could be prevented. Produce such as green leafy vegetables, melons, and oranges are packed with folic acid, and can play a vital role in preventing these birth defects.

Chronic Obstructive Pulmonary Disease

Chronic obstructive pulmonary disease (COPD) is the fourth-leading cause of death in this country, affecting 10 to 20 percent of all adults. COPD covers several conditions, including asthma and bronchitis, each of which affects about 15 million people in the United States each year. Research suggests that a high intake of fruits and vegetables improves a person's breathing function, which reduces their risk of developing these conditions.

Obesity

Today, at least half of the adults in the United States are obese. Obesity is a springboard for an entire range of health problems such as heart disease, high blood pressure, Type 2 diabetes, and high cholesterol. Fruits and vegetables play a part in helping you lose weight and keep it off because they are naturally low in fat and high in fiber—two factors needed for healthy weight loss. If you prepare them healthfully (without large amounts of fat, sugar, or salt), you can often eat large amounts of fruits and vegetables and still lose weight. And the more fruits and vegetables you eat, the less room you'll have for other high-fat, high-calorie foods.

Living the 5 A Day Way

Now that you know about all the health benefits of eating fruits and vegetables, your question is likely to be, how do I make it easy? To make this effort as simple as possible, start with changing your mindset, then work your way to restocking your kitchen. After that, you'll be ready—even excited—to reach your 5 A Day goal.

Change Your Thinking, Change Your Life

When it comes to eating more fruits and vegetables, we all have different hang-ups: Some of us can't imagine spending the time and energy to buy and prepare more fruits and vegetables; others may want to but can't figure out how to break away from the meat-and-potatoes (with special emphasis on meat) meal-planning routine.

The first step to reach your 5 A Day goal is to change the way you think about fruits and vegetables. Need some help to see them in a whole new light? Consider:

You're already halfway there. Think that 5 seems impossible? If you're like most people, you're already getting anywhere from 2.5 to 4.4 servings of fruits and vegetables a day. If you think of it that way, adding 2 to 3 more servings won't be a monumental task. Take an orange as a snack, drink 100 percent vegetable or fruit juice instead of soda, make one of the delicious recipes in this cookbook, and you've made your goal. The 5 A Day way isn't asking you to overhaul the way you live. It requires only a few small

5 A Day Quick Tip

Pack moist towelettes in the car glove compartment, in lunch boxes, and in your purse to wash sticky faces and fingers after a fruit or vegetable snack.

changes here and there to get the overwhelming benefits of eating more fruits and vegetables.

You want what's best for you and your family. If a doctor told you to take medication to treat or prevent disease, you would. If a miracle supplement were invented to keep your family from getting ill, you'd make them take it. Many of us would take any precaution we could to protect and maintain the well-being of our families and ourselves. So why wouldn't you strive for 5 or more servings of fruits and vegetables a day, knowing that this simple step will ensure a healthier life for your whole family?

Instead of viewing the 5 A Day way as a cumbersome change, look at it from a potentially lifesaving angle. This is much more than a shift in what you eat and how you cook; this one move could help you live longer, improve your quality of life, and even save you money by avoiding expensive medications and medical care.

To make it even easier, remember this: Just adding 1 serving a day provides real health benefits. Every new vegetable or fruit that finds its way onto your plate contributes disease-fighting power.

You're worth it. People may pass on fruits and vegetables, claiming that they are too expensive. Yet many of us may not think twice about dropping a few dollars for an ice cream sundae—when that same amount of money could buy you a pint of luscious red raspberries. Put those red raspberries,

Get Your Servings in a Glass

Whether you're working out or just working, you need to keep your body well hydrated to maintain your health and energy. But there's much more than just water available for you to get the fluid you need each day. Try 100 percent fruit and vegetable drinks—along with certain high-water-content fruits—to help you get the hydration you need throughout. The bonus is that you get the water you need, and you work your way to your 5 A Day goal! Try these tasty suggestions:

- Make an orange blast in your blender by whirling orange juice with low-fat vanilla yogurt.
- Try a glass of tomato or vegetable juice with a sprig of celery.
- Add crushed ice made from grapefruit juice to a glass of pineapple juice for an exhilarating treat.
- Enjoy refreshing, juice-filled fruits such as watermelon, orange slices, and grapes for healthy snacks during a workout or workday.

or any expensive fruit or vegetable, in the same category of that sundae: You deserve it. If you're going to splurge on food, go for fruits and vegetables. They're not only tasty treats—they're healthy ones, too.

These are not your mother's vegetables. For some people, just the word *vegetable* makes them think of some grayish-hued carrot mash or overcooked Brussels sprouts that they'd rather hide in their napkins than eat. Unfortunately, it's these bad memories of tasteless, unidentifiable foods that has clouded our view of vegetables as something to be forced down our throats or, better yet, secretly fed to the dog.

Forget that. There's an entire world of delicious vegetables out there for you to discover: broccoli rabe, bok choy, red peppers, kale, yellow squash. And for those old standbys such as carrots and Brussels sprouts, you can steam them with herbs and spices or sauté them with a little oil and garlic.

Maybe nobody ever told you this, but vegetables are naturally delicious. All you need to do is try different types and cooking them different ways to

The Color of Health

Did you know that adding color to your plate may add years to your life? The natural pigments that make fruits and vegetables so colorful can also help protect your body from common diseases and illnesses as you age. Think color! The bright red of ripe tomatoes, strawberries, cherries, and cranberries; the brilliant orange of carrots; the vibrant green of kiwifruit and kale; and the dramatic purple of Concord grapes.

Scientists in labs across the country have made astounding discoveries about the health benefits of highly pigmented fruits and vegetables, which contain disease-fighting compounds called phytonutrients. These powerhouses act as a rogue police force, fighting off free radicals that cause cancer and a host of other enemies that increase your risk of heart disease, diabetes, osteoporosis, and more. Here's just a sampling of the health benefits of eating colorful fruits and vegetables:

- The red in tomatoes helps reduce the risk of heart disease, prostate cancer, and other types of cancers

- The yellow in corn protects against macular degeneration, the number-one cause of blindness in the elderly

- The orange in carrots and sweet potatoes helps prevent heart disease by lowering cholesterol and helps reduce the risk of stroke

- The green in dark, leafy greens helps prevent cancer

- The blue in blueberries helps protect memory and motor function as you age, and helps fight cancer and heart disease

- The purple in Concord grapes and grape juice helps prevent heart disease

So when you're filling your shopping cart or your plate, think the more color, the better!

bring our their flavor and entice your tastebuds. Open yourself up to this new world of variety. Before you know it, you'll find yourself longing for a tasty vegetable dish.

It's really a game. Instead of viewing getting 5 or more a day as an obstacle to overcome, see it as a game you want to win. Each day, challenge yourself to get 5 or more servings of fruits and vegetables. If that's too much in the beginning, just try to beat the number of servings you had the day before. Give yourself a point for each serving, then add them up at the end of the day. Keep score and chart your progress. Maybe even give yourself a little treat of a new CD or a kitchen tool for making your goal several days in a row.

Do you have family members who are balking at the idea of eating more fruits and vegetables? Make it a game for them, too, and see who can eat the most each day. Friendly competition will surely spur them on to get more fruits and vegetables in their diets. And this is one game where everyone wins!

Making It Happen

To make eating 5 or more a day a reality, you need a game plan. Even if you've changed the way you think about fruits and vegetables, without a daily and weekly plan of action, you might not follow through despite your best intentions. The following maps out what you need to do today, tomorrow, and each week so that you make your goal of 5 or more a day—every day.

Study what you're doing now. Before you figure out what changes you have to make, first you need to know where you're starting out. For the next few days, study each meal. How many fruit and vegetable servings are you eating with each one? What's your total at the end of the day? (For examples of what's considered a serving, see "What Is a Serving?" on page 14.)

Maybe you'll be shocked to find that you're not that far off at all. Or, maybe you think that you're a healthy eater, but once you calculate it, you're surprised to learn that you don't even come close. But at least now you have your starting point, and you know exactly how far you have to go.

Plan a transition time. If you've been eating only a serving or two a day, you'll overwhelm yourself if you decide to climb all the way to 5 tomorrow and start making vegetable-only dinners. It's that overwhelming feeling that keeps people away from the 5 A Day program.

So make it easy. Give yourself a week or two to gradually increase the amount of fruits and vegetables you eat in a day. Don't worry about elaborate recipes or exotic fruits. Think simply about each meal. Ask yourself: Can I have fruit for a snack today? Can I slice bananas on my cereal this morning? Can I put more lettuce and tomatoes on my sandwich for lunch? Once you get that down, then you can progress to new recipes and produce. But this will get you started simply and easily. When you see how easy it is, you'll be motivated to strive for more.

Let fruits and vegetables take center stage. In the typical American meal, fruits and vegetables have a supporting role. The meat takes the center of the plate, and the vegetable side dishes are chosen to complement the meat.

In the 5 A Day way, you turn that thinking around. When planning a meal, think of your fruit and vegetable selections first. Then, if you feel you even need meat, let the meat portion of your plate take the spot that the vegetables used to hold: as a small side dish. And try to have lean, skinless chicken or fish occupy that spot.

You can even expand this theory to dining out. If you're going to a buffet, load up your plate with fruits and vegetables first. Then in whatever little space you have left, add some meat.

It may take some time to make this way of planning meals a habit, but within weeks, you'll automatically start arranging your meals around fruits and vegetables.

Have a fruit or vegetable with every meal. Include a fruit and vegetable every time you eat, and you'll find that it's easy to reach 5 or more servings. And if you focus on one meal at a time, you won't feel overwhelmed. To really hit the mark, double up on servings at one meal or more and always use snack time as a fruit-and-veggie time.

Keep it easy. There's never been an easier time to get more fruits and vegetables in your diet. You can

What Is a Serving?

If 5 servings a day sounds like a lot you, you'll be happy to find that it doesn't take much to make a serving. Did you eat an apple today? That's one. Six ounces of OJ with breakfast? That's two. A side salad with lunch? That's three. Once you know what a serving size is, you'll find that you may already be close to getting your 5 or more a day. Here are some examples of common serving sizes:

1	medium-size fruit
¾	cup (6 oz) 100 percent fruit or vegetable juice
¼	cup dried fruit
½	cup cooked, frozen, or canned vegetables or fruit
1	cup raw leafy vegetables
½	cup cooked dry peas or beans

5 a day: the better health plan

buy prewashed, prepackaged salad mixes with a variety of veggies and greens; you can snack on prepeeled baby carrots; you can feast on individual-size cans of fruit; and portable fruits such as apples, oranges, pears, and grapes, which have always been nature's own fast food.

So don't make getting 5 or more a day any harder than it has to be. Take advantage of these easy-to-eat options. Then, when you have time, make more elaborate dishes where you cut and prepare the fruits and vegetables yourself.

Plan out your week. Everyone is so busy these days, the idea of making meals that are rich in fruits and vegetables each day may seem daunting. But if you set aside just an hour each weekend to map out your week, you'll find that you can save time and make your 5 A Day goal with little effort.

Each Saturday or Sunday, sketch out your meals. Then go to the market to get the ingredients you need. It doesn't even have to be completely thought-out: You can have an idea that you'll have a casserole on Monday, some kind of pasta dish on Tuesday, and so on. But at least if you have a concept, you won't be scrambling for ingredients at 6:00 on a weeknight, only to get frustrated and then order an unhealthy take-out dinner.

If you really want to make your week go easier, try preparing as much as you can on the weekend. Make casseroles or vegetable soups and freeze them. Cut and prepare vegetables and then blanch them so that they stay fresh until you need them later in the week. Cut up carrots, celery, and peppers and keep them in a zip-top bag for a snack or as an add-in for salads and stir-fries.

Let go of "fresh is the only option." Some people fall into the idea that if it isn't fresh produce, then it isn't good for you—or good-tasting.

The good news is that canned and frozen produce are terrific options with about the same nutritional content as fresh. In fact, frozen vegetables are flash-frozen after being harvested, so their nutrients are locked in. They're considered equal in nutrition to fresh produce, and oftentimes, they're already chopped, so that saves you another step. So when you're out shopping, don't shy away from canned or frozen vegetables and fruits. Do the opposite: Stock up on them because they can make hitting your goal of 5 or more servings a day easier than ever.

Keep them around. Leave oranges, bananas, and apples in a bowl on the counter. Put precut fruits and vegetables in the refrigerator ready to eat—and in plain view, not hidden in the crisper. If fruits and vegetables are all around you, you'll be more likely to pick them up for a snack or to add them to a meal. If they are out of the way, or if they take too much effort to prepare, you'll pass them up for a bag of chips or a piece of candy.

Focus on color and appearance. Good foods have much more than good taste. We like to eat attractive foods—those with colors and textures that please our eyes as well as our tastebuds. And nothing could be more visually appealing than the luscious red of a bell pepper, the deep blue hue of blueberries, and the bright orange of a tangerine. Instead of viewing them as a health necessity, look at fruits and vegetables as tools to make any meal more appealing to the eye. Once you can do that, you'll notice that you're adding colorful produce everywhere to make each meal a feast for the eyes.

Buy one new produce item each week. Some research suggests that people buy the same 20 food items each week. That may seem convenient, but it puts us in a rut that keeps us from experiencing the many different varieties out there. While you do want to expand your produce universe, you don't want to overhaul your buying habits to the point where you find yourself overwhelmed with new foods and new recipes.

To keep your sanity and expand your produce horizons at the same time, buy one new produce item each week. Try bok choy one week, clementines the next, and so on. Then, as you learn to like each new introduction, that item will become part of your standard purchases, and you'll gradually build up an arsenal of fruits and vegetables in your meal regimen.

Do your homework. It might have seemed like a great idea to buy a mango at the supermarket, but now that you're home, just what do you do with it? You don't know, so you let it sit and rot. Or it tastes awful because it wasn't ripe yet. Or you try to do something with it and it turns into a disaster. So now you're sour on mangoes.

This scenario is easily avoidable with just a little research. Before you buy fruits and vegetables that you have little experience with, do some simple, fun homework. Start by reading cookbooks or magazines, or ask people in the produce section of the supermarket for buying and serving ideas. Sometimes, you'll find consumer tip sheets or information cards (often with recipes) tucked into produce displays. Watch cooking shows to get a firsthand look at how top chefs use various fruits and vegetables.

Another research option is www.aboutproduce.com, a site brought to you by the Produce Marketing Association and the Produce for Better Health Foundation. Here you'll find a ton of information about fruits and vegetables. This database tells you how to buy them, store them, and prepare them. You'll also learn about nutritional benefits, fat and calorie counts, and what parts of certain fruits and vegetables you can and cannot eat.

For example, if you looked up mangoes, you'd learn that they come in six different varieties, and that you should avoid bruised and shriveled fruit. When buying, look for full and somewhat firm fruit with taut skin and a strong aroma. If a mango is unripe, keep it on your countertop; if it's ripe, refrigerate. Mangoes must be peeled, and you can eat only the flesh, which has a sweet flavor and smooth texture. After that, you'll find serving tips (like mango salsa) and several mango recipes. Before you know it, you'll be a mango expert!

Eat out. Here's a fun way to do homework—go to your favorite restaurants. Order all kinds of fruits and vegetables prepared all sorts of ways. This

Delicious Desserts in a Flash

It may sound like a dream come true, but dessert can actually help you get to 5 or more servings a day. What better way to top off a meal than to use luscious—and healthy—fruits to complement your desserts! Try these sweet suggestions:

- Serve baked apples or pears.
- Serve fresh fruit with chunks of reduced-fat cheese. Use an apple corer to help make easy, perfect wedges.
- Fill meringue shells with fresh or frozen fruits. Top with berries or pureed fruit.
- Top melon wedges with a small scoop of fruit sorbet or top with a sauce made from pureed raspberries.
- Top angel food or pound cake with seasonal fruits and garnish with a bunch of frosty frozen grapes.
- Serve assorted dried fruit like dates, figs, prunes, raisins, and apricots with low-fat cookies.

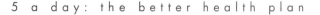

kind of field trip is a great way to figure out which ones you like, don't like, and how you like them cooked. Feel free to ask the chef how she prepared them so that you can try it yourself.

To further expand your fruit and vegetable outlook, go to ethnic restaurants such as Chinese, Mexican, Thai, and French. You'll be exposed to a whole new world of produce and preparation that you'll be able to use in your daily meal planning.

The 5 A Day Kitchen Makeover

Once you take the mental steps necessary to live the 5 A Day way, then it's time to physically set yourself up for success. When your kitchen is stocked with everything you need, getting 5 or more servings of fruits and vegetables a day is a breeze.

So give your kitchen a makeover. When you're all stocked up, you'll find that you'll never lack the ingredients or utensils you need to eat 5 or more servings a day. From the refrigerator to the pantry to the countertops, here's how to prepare your kitchen.

What to Keep in Your Workspace

The real beauty of fruits and vegetables is that they require very little preparation. So you don't have to overhaul your supply of kitchenware to make delicious produce dishes. But if you want to maximize the way you serve and prepare fruits and vegetables, keep a few of the following devices and culinary tools around. They'll make your life easier and expand your meal-planning horizons.

Crock-Pot/slow cooker. Short of having a hired cook, a Crock-Pot, or slow cooker, is the best appliance to help you have dinner ready the minute you walk in the door after a long day at work. In the morning, toss all the ingredients in, and when you get home at night, dinner is ready. Fill the pot up with vegetables and a bit of meat, or make vegetable stews or soups.

Fat-free cooking spray or an oil mister. These will allow you to sauté vegetables and grease roasting or baking pans without adding much fat.

Food processor/blender. These handy devices make chopping, pureeing, and shredding fruits and vegetables a simple task. A blender also allows you to make fruit smoothies—another fun and easy way to sneak fruits into your daily diet.

Herbs and spices. With just a dash of some common herbs and spices, you can transform plain vegetables into a culinary marvel. Keep a full arsenal in your spice rack, and you'll never want for ways to prepare various vegetables. Strong-flavored herbs include bay leaf, caraway, fennel, sweet marjoram, oregano, rosemary, sage, savory, and thyme. Moderate-flavored herbs include chives, dill, and mint. Delicate herbs include basil, chervil, cilantro, and parsley. (For more on how to use herbs and spices with fruits and vegetables, see "Spice It Up.")

Juicer. If you like to be hands-on, a juicer is a fun way to hit your 5 A Day goal. Toss in celery, tomatoes, carrots, and other vegetables to make your own juice cocktail, or enjoy a glass of fresh orange or grapefruit juice each morning.

Spice It Up

Add the exotic and extraordinary to everyday vegetables and meals with herbs and spices. With all your herb and spice choices, however, you may not know which flavorful additions go best with certain foods. Here's a general guide to what herbs and spices go well with different fruits, vegetables, and dishes.

Basil: Good with tomatoes and tomato products, pasta, cabbage, carrots, onions, squash, beans, salad dressings, and soups.

Chives: Good for vegetable mixtures, salads and dressings, omelets, and soups.

Cilantro: Leaves are good for Mexican and Chinese cooking. Seeds are useful with pea soup, salads, eggs, mushrooms, pickles, salads, and soups.

Dill: Used in pickled cucumbers and other vegetables. Mix dill with yogurt to top fish, vegetables, or pasta.

Fennel: Use in any apple or tomato dish, sauces, and soups. Good in lentil and dried bean dishes.

Garlic: Use for sauces, dressings, tomatoes, and green vegetables. Rub a cut clove on the surface of a salad bowl before adding tossed salad. Add after browning onions for soups and stews. Sprinkle browned garlic over cooked fresh vegetables.

Marjoram: Good with foods such as soups, stews, potatoes, pasta, rice, and vegetables.

Mint: Use fresh leaves in fruit and vegetable salads or as a garnish for summer's creamy fruit soups.

Oregano: Add to beans, sauces, soups, and fresh mushrooms. It enhances any tomato dish.

Parsley: Stir into soups, sauces, salads, mashed potatoes, and marinades. Sprinkle chopped parsley over hot cooked rice, vegetables, pasta, and potatoes.

Thyme: Adds flavor to chowders, marinades, tomato sauce, pasta, rice, and most vegetables, especially potatoes, mushrooms, and tomatoes.

Microwave oven. A busy person's best friend, a microwave helps you cook vegetables fast while keeping their bright color, fresh taste, and crisp texture. Microwaving can help retain nutrients too, if a minimum amount of water is used. Even leftover vegetables come out as flavorful as the first time around. (For more tips on microwaving vegetables, see "The Microwave Way to 5 A Day" on page 23.)

Steamer. While you can steam vegetables in a microwave, some people love the quickness and performance of an actual steamer. Add a few spices or a squeeze of lemon, and you'll have tasty vegetables cooked to perfection in no time. If you don't want to purchase a steamer, opt for a steamer basket to place in a skillet or saucepan.

Wok/stir-fry pan. There's no easier to way to make a quick meal than throwing a bunch of cut vegetables (or packaged frozen veggie mixes) into a wok or stir-fry pan with some leftover chicken or meat. It cooks quickly, so foods retain their nutrients, but requires only a little bit of oil. If you prefer, you can use any good nonstick pan to make these skillet sensations.

What to Keep in Your Refrigerator

If your refrigerator is stocked up right, you'll always be ready to make a quick salad, grab a nice snack, or cook up something delicious.

Apples, oranges, and grapefruit. These will keep for weeks in this cool setting.

Fresh vegetables and fruits. Stock only what you plan to use in the next 3 to 4 days. After that, they may spoil.

Prewashed and prepared salad mix bags. Make a quick salad, or add them to sandwiches.

Baby carrots. Cut them and cook them, add them to salads, toss them into soups and stews, or just dip them in low-fat salad dressing as a snack. They're the perfect all-purpose vegetable.

Orange juice. A great way to start the day, OJ is also a nice addition to homemade salad dressings, dessert toppings, and some recipes. You can even use it instead of oil to sauté vegetables.

100 percent vegetable juice. Try this refresher as a healthy yet tasty alternative to soda.

What to Keep in Your Freezer

As we said earlier, frozen vegetables and fruits are not only good for you, they can also make getting 5 or more servings a day a snap. And with a well-stocked freezer, you can have just about any type of fruit or vegetable no matter what season it is.

Frozen strawberries, raspberries, blueberries, and peeled bananas. Dead of winter? You still can have these delectable fruits if you keep them in your freezer. Blend them with some yogurt and orange juice to make a smoothie, or puree them to make a fruit topping for dessert. Or just let them thaw and enjoy them as is.

Frozen vegetables and vegetable mixes. There's a seemingly endless variety of vegetables in the frozen food section of your supermarket. Have these on hand to make a stir-fry meal, or add them to noodle, pasta, bean, and rice dishes to boost the vegetable content. With these on hand, you can have an easy vegetable-rich meal any time.

Pizza shells. Stash these in your freezer, and you can have a homemade gourmet pizza in a snap—without calling for take-out. Just thaw slightly, then top with tomato sauce, fresh or frozen vegetables, and some low-fat cheese for a fun and healthy meal.

Veggie burgers. These tasty patties come in a variety of flavors and can be cooked up quickly. Even if you don't want to replace tried-and-true burgers, veggie burgers make a great change-of-pace lunch or dinner.

What to Keep in Your Pantry

Every chef knows that a well-stocked pantry means you can whip up a good meal at any time. And the chef in a 5 A Day kitchen knows that a well-stocked pantry means that you can create a fruit- and vegetable-filled good meal at any time. Keep the following in your pantry, and you'll never have to say "There's nothing to eat" ever again.

Canned beans. Toss them in with rice or pasta and a variety of vegetables, make bean burritos filled with lettuce, tomato, and salsa, and throw them into vegetable soups to make them more hearty. Stock a good mix: baked beans, black beans, chickpeas, kidney beans, lentils, lima beans, pinto beans, and split peas.

Canned corn. An easy side dish, but corn can also be added to soups, stews, and chilies, and even to salsas to make a more interesting dip.

Canned fruits. Keep canned peaches, fruit cup, pineapples, and pears around for easy-to-carry snacks or for dessert toppings.

Canned green beans and peas. Another easy side dish, these can also be mixed in with soups, casseroles, and other meals.

Canned and jarred soups. There's a wealth of vegetable-rich ready-to-serve soups available in stores now. Some even come with pop-off tops, so you can take a can to work and microwave it. If you want to increase the vegetable content even more, add a can of corn or peas to the soup.

Dried fruits. Use them as a snack or toss them into dough or batter for baked goods. And they're great tossed with cereal in a homemade trail mix.

Onions. These versatile favorites are easy to sauté and add to meat and chicken dishes, stir-fries, or any type of vegetable blend. You can also add them to sandwiches, burgers, and stews.

Pastas. Keep a variety of shapes and sizes. Pasta makes it easy to serve any type of vegetables. Cover it in tomato sauce, then add sautéed onions, zucchini, carrots, and peppers for an easy pasta primavera.

Salsa. A healthy dip for vegetables and chips, this versatile product can be added to vegetable mixes, omelets, Mexican meals, or bean dishes to add taste as well as health-protecting nutrients.

Sauces and marinades. Stock up on soy, teriyaki, barbecue, and honey-mustard sauces as well as flavored vinegars (use sparingly, however, as these sauces generally have a high salt content). Even if you cook the same vegetables each night, these condiments can give them an entirely new taste.

Tomato sauce and canned tomatoes. With these around, you have an easy vegetable addition to any pasta dish. But you can also use these for stir-fries, homemade veggie pizzas, and vegetable lasagna. You can even buy canned tomatoes with onions, garlic, and chili spices already added to give your meals an extra kick.

Tortillas. You can wrap just about any bean or vegetable filling in this low-fat Mexican bread for a quick and easy lunch or dinner. Or, top a tortilla with low-sodium tomato sauce or salsa, sliced vegetables, and shredded low-fat cheese for a healthy mini-pizza.

The 5 A Day Meal Makeovers

Each meal and snack isn't just a time to eat in the 5 A Day program—it's an opportunity to get yet another serving of fruits and vegetables. With a simple addition or a small change to each mealtime, you can make your 5 or more goal an easy reality. Try some of the following ideas for each meal:

The Microwave Way to 5 A Day

Vegetables are a dream when cooked in the microwave. These foods retain all of their bright color, fresh taste, and crisp texture when cooked in a microwave. Microwaving can help retain nutrients too, if a minimum amount of water is used. Even leftover vegetables come out as flavorful as the first time around. And, by microwaving in a serving dish, there's no pot to clean up.

Whether you're making a serving for one or for a dinner party, your microwave can make it fast and easy to prepare vegetables. Here are some tips for success:

- Use only microwaveable containers.
- For even cooking, cut vegetables into same-size pieces.
- Stir or rotate a half-turn halfway through cooking.
- Loosely cover foods so that steam can escape, using waxed paper, microwaveable plastic wrap, or the cooking container's lid.
- Use a fork to pierce whole, unpeeled vegetables or fruits such as potatoes, sweet potatoes, and apples to keep them from bursting while cooking.
- Follow package directions for cooking frozen vegetables.
- Remove vegetables from the microwave oven when they are barely tender; let stand 3 to 5 minutes to finish cooking. Be careful not to burn yourself when removing covers, as microwaved foods produce hot steam.

Breakfast

- Slice bananas and strawberries over cereal.
- Top cereal and plain yogurt with cut or canned fruit.
- Eat a slice of melon with your bagel with light cream cheese.
- Spread strawberry, kiwi, banana slices, or blueberries over waffles and French toast.
- Make an omelet with chopped (possibly even leftover!) onions, mushrooms, peppers, zucchini, and spinach.
- Add dried fruit to plain yogurt or cereal.
- Blend a breakfast smoothie. Toss in chopped or frozen fruit with fat-free milk or low-fat yogurt. Add low-fat granola or your favorite cereal for added texture.
- Fill half a honeydew melon with blueberries and top it with a squeeze of lime.

Lunch

- Take a ready-to-serve vegetable soup (from the store, or one you made yourself).
- Head to the salad bar and fill up on mostly raw vegetables. Take some home to save yourself chopping time for dinner.
- Add extra tomato slices, onions, and lettuce or spinach to sandwiches. Use that in place of half the meat. Experiment with different types of lettuce: red leaf, romaine, Bibb, or endive.
- Add fruit chunks to regular lettuce salads.
- Order a baked potato but have it covered in chives and broccoli instead of cheese and butter. Or, microwave one yourself and top with low-fat cheese, tomato sauce, and pepper slices.
- Buy or make a bean burrito stuffed with extra vegetables.
- Chop up leftover cooked chicken and mix with yogurt, apples, grapes, raisins, pineapple, celery, carrots, cucumber, radishes, and zucchini. Eat as is or stuff into a whole wheat pita for a chicken salad sandwich.

5 a day: the better health plan

Dinner

- Stir chunked fresh vegetables or a frozen blend into regular jarred tomato sauce and serve over pasta.
- Use fruit as an edible garnish—grapes on a sole fillet, pineapple slices on an oriental chicken breast.
- If you're already making a casserole, mix in extra vegetables.
- Throw any type of vegetable in a food processor, sauté, then add to lasagna.
- Cut up bell peppers, broccoli, onions, garlic, and mushrooms to top a pizza crust spread with tomato sauce.
- Coat vegetables with a bit of olive oil, thread them on a skewer, and cook on the grill. You also can grill pineapple as a dessert.
- Make a meat loaf stuffed with celery, onions, carrots, and lentils.

Kids Do Love Fruits and Vegetables!

You may be sold on the 5 A Day way, but something tells you that your picky 4-year-old is going to have a completely different idea about it. It's important that you get your kids eating 5 or more fruits and vegetables a day. Research shows that children are lagging behind their adult counterparts by a full serving.

How to do the impossible? Try these kid-tested strategies to get your little ones to eat more produce.

Keep trying. Ever notice how kids hate green beans one day and love them the next? One expert says that you need to offer a food 12 times to a child before he will learn to like it. So don't take "yuck" as the final answer.

Serve them fresh. Foods sometimes taste more bitter to children than adults. Raw vegetables don't have quite as bitter a taste. And kids also prefer things that crunch—the more noise the better—to softer, cooked vegetables.

Let 'em dip. Find low-fat dips—either salad dressings or dips in the produce department—for vegetables. And feel free to try caramel or chocolate dips for fruit. (Just serve in moderation.) You'll be surprised at how many fruits and vegetables kids will eat if they have something messy to dip them in.

Play with their food. Here's an afternoon project: Make "cars" by filling celery sticks with peanut butter, using cut carrot coins as wheels, and raisins on the top of the peanut butter for people. Or make smiley faces with blueberries and bananas on pancakes. Anything you can do to make eating fruits and vegetables silly and fun increases your chances of getting kids to eat them.

Let them choose. Every time you take them to the market, tell them they can pick one fruit or vegetable. Encourage them to choose different colors, textures, and shapes. Then when you get home, let them help you prepare the food so they feel like they're part of the process. They'll be thrilled to eat something they helped choose and prepare.

Lead by example. If you eat fruits and vegetables, they eventually will, and they'll learn healthy habits that will stay with them for a lifetime.

- Cut a butternut squash in half and cook it in the microwave for a few minutes, until it's fork-tender. Top with a pat of butter and your favorite herbs and spices for a great main or side dish.
- Make a no-lettuce vegetable salad with sliced carrots, broccoli, cucumbers, and peppers. Add some cooked beans and experiment with different flavored vinegars.

Snacks

- Freeze pureed fruit to make juice bars or ice cubes. Or, freeze grapes and eat them as a cold treat.
- Eat an apple or a banana instead of heading to the vending machine.
- Eat a bowl of fresh berries as a nighttime snack.
- Dip baby carrots in low-fat salad dressing.
- Cut up carrots, peppers, and celery sticks and munch on them throughout the day.
- Open an individual-size can of pineapple, peaches, or fruit cup.

Simple Stir-In Ideas

This cookbook is packed with great recipes and ideas for getting more fruits and vegetables in your meals. But inevitably, there will be times when you can't think of an easy way to fit them in. For those moments, try some of the following simple stir-in ideas.

- Stir chopped and sautéed vegetables into grain and rice dishes.
- Add a bit of chopped orange or fresh grated ginger while vegetables are cooking. Add salsa or a drizzle of lemon or lime juice just before serving.
- Toss dried fruit, chives, or scallions into couscous or pasta.
- For a quick fruit salad, empty a can of juice-packed mandarin oranges into a bowl, then add one sliced banana, one cut-up apple, and some frozen blueberries.
- Add extra vegetables like tomatoes, parsnips, cauliflower, peppers, and new potatoes to stews and dishes such as chicken cacciatore.
- Tear open a salad in a bag and combine with chunks of fruit or last night's leftover chicken, beef, or fish.

a week's worth of·5 a day menus

For many people, one of the most challenging aspects of trying to eat five or more servings of fruits and vegetables a day is figuring out how to integrate those servings into their regular meal routine.

The 7-Day Menu Plan below illustrates a key secret of the 5 A Day program: When you incorporate more fruits and vegetables into your diet, you naturally eliminate other foods that are less healthy and nutrient-dense.

We created this plan so that each day, no more than four or five dishes require following a formal recipe. These dishes are followed by a page reference in parentheses, such as (Recipe: page 56), to direct you to the recipe. Some menus are then rounded out with suggestions from Quick Cook boxes. Again, page references are given, such as (Quick Cook: page 83). Other items in the menus are prepared from foods commonly found in the pantry and refrigerator.

Note that each day's menu plan is followed by "Number of 5 A Day servings" to help you see how many fruit and vegetable servings you would get were you to prepare the whole day's menus. We also encourage you to mix and match menus, trying dishes from different menus on different days. The point is to have fun with it—with the extra bonus of increasing your intake of fruits and vegetables. You're certain to learn some great new ways to create meals, and you'll enjoy the new healthy you.

M o n d a y

Breakfast
Island Shake (Recipe: page 50)
Rice cakes

Lunch
Apple-Fennel Soup (Recipe: page 88)
Lemony Bean Salad (Recipe: page 116)
Whole-grain roll

Snack
Low-fat cottage cheese and raspberries

Dinner
Mixed greens with dressing
Cioppino (Recipe: page 161)
Sourdough bread
Roasted Pears with Honey (Quick Cook: page 224)

Snack
Raisins and peanuts

Number of 5 A Day servings: 9.5

T u e s d a y

Breakfast
100% orange juice (6 ounces)
Dried Fruit and Almond Granola with Yogurt and Banana (Recipe: page 39)

Lunch
Mediterranean Pasta Salad (Recipe: page 114)
Onion and rosemary focaccia
Sliced strawberries and peaches

Snack
Dried apricots

Dinner
Pork Tenderloin with Orange-Basil Sauce (Recipe: page 156)
Soba noodles or linguine with toasted sesame seeds
Steamed green beans with fresh parsley
Plumberry Granita (Recipe: page 218)

Number of 5 A Day servings: 9

Wednesday

Breakfast
Rio Breakfast Shake (Recipe: page 51)
Low-fat raisin bran muffin

Lunch
Tuna, white bean, and red onion salad
Sesame bread sticks
Low-sodium iced tomato juice with celery (6 ounces)

Snack
Low-fat yogurt with fresh blueberries

Dinner
Sautéed mushrooms on grilled country bread
Bowties with Tomato-Pepper Sauce (Recipe: page 141)
Tuscan-Style Spinach (Quick Cook: page 120)
Spiced Peach and Dried Plum Compote (Recipe: page 219)

Snack
Northwest Pear Slush (Recipe: page 48)

Number of 5 A Day servings: 13.5

Thursday

Breakfast
100% red grape juice (6 ounces)
Cinnamon Oatmeal with Fruit and Nuts (Recipe: page 40)
Whole grain toast with low-fat cheese or cream cheese

Lunch
South of the Border Squash Soup (Recipe: page 94)
Seven-grain bread
Tomato and watercress salad
Grapefruit Fizz (Recipe: page 46)

Snack
Frozen Grapes (Quick Cook: page 220)

Dinner
Red and yellow cherry tomato salad
Grilled Turkey-Mushroom Burgers with Chutney Sauce (Recipe: page 153)
Pan-Roasted Potatoes (Quick Cook: Page 186)
Warm Blueberry Cobbler (Recipe: page 216)

Snack
Banana

Number of 5 A Day servings: 11.5

Friday

Breakfast

100% orange-tangerine juice (6 ounces)
Applesauce with Crunchy Topping (Recipe: page 38)
Toasted low-fat corn-blueberry muffin

Lunch

Health Salad Sandwich (Quick Cook: page 119)
Fresh strawberries with mint
Lemon-ginger iced tea

Snack

Plain popcorn

Dinner

Spinach-Citrus Salad (Recipe: page 123)
Fruited Chicken Paprika (Recipe: page 149)
Steamed new potatoes
Yellow and green summer squash
Chocolate sorbet

Snack

Any-Fruit Smoothie (Quick Cook: page 48)

Number of 5 A Day servings: 13

Saturday

Breakfast

100% cranberry-apple juice (6 ounces)
Grapefruit with brown sugar
Tomato, Garlic, and Pesto Omelet (Recipe: page 44)
Whole grain toast

Lunch

Orange, black olive, and arugula salad
Governor's Black Bean Soup (Recipe: page 89)
Watermelon-Lime Slush (12 ounces); (Quick Cook: page 46)

Snack

Dried cherries and peanuts

Dinner

Tomato and Red Onion Salad (Quick Cook: page 121)
Baked Manicotti with Asparagus (Recipe: page 138)
Garlic bread
Italian Fruit Cobbler with Vanilla Sauce (Recipe: page 222)

Number of 5 A Day servings: 12

Brunch

100% freshly squeezed blood orange juice (6 ounces)
Sweet Potato Pancakes with Apple-Walnut Topping (Recipe: page 43)
California Fruit Salad (Recipe: page 109)
Toasted pita
Sparkling water with lime

Snack

Frozen nonfat yogurt with sliced banana

Dinner

Steamed asparagus with lemon wedges
Baked Almond Sole with Warm Wild Rice Salad (Recipe: page 170)
Pear-Strawberry Trifle (Recipe: page 223)

Number of 5 A Day servings: 12

5 a day
power menus

With today's busy lifestyle, it can sometimes be hard, even impossible, to prepare breakfast, lunch, and dinner in your kitchen. A great alternative is to target one meal a day, such as a weeknight dinner or a leisurely weekend lunch, to pack your five servings into one meal. Here are seven suggestions. In addition to each providing five or more produce servings, they are designed with one top priority in mind: great flavor and irresistible combinations of fruits and vegetables, along with pasta, meat, poultry, and fish and seafood. You'll find menus for your family, for entertaining, even a menu prepared completely on the grill.

No more than three dishes in each menu require following a formal recipe from the book. These dishes are followed by a page reference in parentheses, such as (Recipe: page 56), to direct you to the recipe. Some menus are then rounded out with suggestions from Quick Cook boxes, also with page references given, such as (Quick Cook: page 83). Other items in the menus are prepared from foods commonly found in the pantry and refrigerator.

As you plan your weekly shopping, choose one or two of the power menus each week, and purchase the ingredients you need ahead of time. After familiarizing yourself with the Power Menus and the other recipes in this book, you may just find yourself creating your own Power Menus. Bon appétit!

Menu 1

Bartlett Pear and Mango Salsa (Recipe: page 81)
Baked corn chips
Avocado and Smoked Turkey Salad in Bread Baskets (Recipe: page 134)
Crispy Beer-Batter Onion Rings (Recipe: page 184)
Angel food cake with topped berries and nondairy whipped topping

Number of 5 A Day servings: 5

Menu 2

Watermelon Gazpacho (Recipe: page 97)
Pasta with Cherry Tomatoes and Parsley (Quick Cook: page 140)
Steamed broccoli with lemon wedges
Seeded bread sticks
One-Ingredient Sorbet (Quick Cook: page 215)

Number of 5 A Day servings: 7

Menu 3

Chilled Nectarine Soup (Recipe: page 91)
Broiled or grilled skewered shrimp
Garden-Style Risotto (Recipe: page 210)
Caramelized Onions (Recipe: page 183)
Cantaloupe wedges with fresh raspberries

Number of 5 A Day servings: 6

Menu 4

White Bean and Garlic Spread (Quick Cook: page 81)
Three-lettuce salad with dressing
Polenta, Spinach, and Mushroom Lasagna (Recipe: page 209) with tomato sauce
Frozen nonfat vanilla yogurt with Chunky Northwest Pear and Fig Sauce
(Recipe: page 221)

Number of 5 A Day servings: 7.5

Menu 5

Cold Honeydew-Lime Soup (Recipe: page 90)
Broiled pork tenderloin with teriyaki sauce
Kiwifruit-Mango Salsa (Recipe: page 80)
Farmer's Market Black Bean, Corn, and Tomato Salad (Quick Cook: page 117)
Watermelon wedges with lime

Number of 5 A Day servings: 5

Menu 6

Cool Summer Gazpacho Salad (Recipe: page 121)
Grilled chicken breasts
Citrus Slaw (Recipe: page 117)
Grilled rosemary potatoes
Brown Sugar Grilled Peaches (Quick Cook: page 219)

Number of 5 A Day servings: 6

Menu 7

Asparagus and Blood Orange Salad (Recipe: page 115)
Broiled salmon
Green Beans with Tomato, Basil, and Goat Cheese (Recipe: page 177)
Corn on the cob
Northwest Cherry and Tropical Fruit Salad (Recipe: page 102)

Number of 5 A Day servings: 8.5

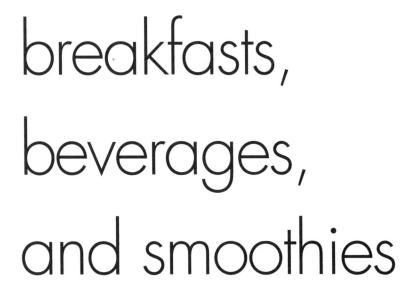

breakfasts, beverages, and smoothies

applesauce with crunchy topping

¾	cup bran flakes
2	tablespoons finely chopped pecans
3	tablespoons firmly packed brown sugar
1	tablespoon margarine or butter
2	cups applesauce

In a medium bowl, combine the bran flakes and pecans. In a large saucepan, heat the brown sugar and margarine over medium heat until melted and smooth. Remove from the heat; add the bran mixture, tossing to coat evenly. Cool completely. Spoon the applesauce into dessert dishes and top with the bran mixture.

Makes 4 servings
Per serving: 157 calories; 1.3 g protein; 27.6 g carbohydrate; 5.4 g fat; 0 mg cholesterol; 2.9 g dietary fiber; 19 mg sodium

Number of 5 A Day servings: 1

blueberry-pineapple parfaits

1	can (20 ounces) pineapple chunks, drained
1	container (8 ounces) fat-free lemon-flavored yogurt
1½	cups fresh blueberries or frozen blueberries, thawed and patted dry
½	cup granola

In a small bowl, combine the pineapple with half of the yogurt. In small wineglasses or juice glasses, alternately layer the pineapple-yogurt mixture, blueberries, and granola. Repeat the layering twice. Top each parfait with a dollop of yogurt.

Makes 4 servings
Per serving: 233 calories; 4 g protein; 49 g carbohydrate; 3 g fat; 0 mg cholesterol; 3.2 g dietary fiber; 43 mg sodium

Number of 5 A Day servings: 1.5

dried fruit and almond granola with yogurt and banana

3	tablespoons firmly packed brown sugar
3	tablespoons honey
1¼	teaspoons light sesame oil
¼	teaspoon ground cinnamon
¼	teaspoon vanilla extract
¼	teaspoon almond extract
2	cups old-fashioned oats
⅓	cup sesame seeds
½	cup whole natural almonds
⅓	cup sliced almonds
⅓	cup dried cranberries
⅓	cup golden raisins
	Fat-free vanilla yogurt and 4 bananas, sliced, for serving

Place an oven rack in the middle of the oven and preheat oven to 350°F. Coat a rimmed baking sheet with cooking spray.

In a heavy medium saucepan, combine the brown sugar, honey, sesame oil, cinnamon, and vanilla and almond extracts. Cook over low heat, stirring, just until the sugar melts; remove from the heat. Add the oats and sesame seeds, stirring until coated. Spread evenly on the prepared baking sheet.

Bake for 10 minutes. Stir, then sprinkle the whole and sliced almonds over the top. Bake for 10 minutes longer, or until the almonds are lightly toasted. Cool completely in the pan. Transfer the granola to a large bowl and stir in the cranberries and raisins. Store in an airtight container up to 2 weeks.

To serve, spoon ½ cup yogurt into a bowl and top with ½ cup granola and ½ sliced banana.

Makes 8 servings
Per serving: 423 calories; 12.1 g protein; 69.8 g carbohydrate; 11.9 g fat; 2.8 mg cholesterol; 7.2 g dietary fiber; 78 mg sodium

Number of 5 A Day servings: 1

cinnamon oatmeal
with fruit and nuts

6	ounces grapefruit juice
¾	cup water
¼	teaspoon ground cinnamon
⅛	teaspoon salt
⅔	cup old-fashioned oats
2	tablespoons firmly packed brown sugar
2	oranges or tangerines, sectioned
2	tablespoons chopped dates
1	tablespoon sliced almonds, toasted

In a medium saucepan, combine the grapefruit juice, water, cinnamon, and salt; bring to a boil over high heat. Stir in the oats and reduce the heat to medium-low. Cook for 5 minutes, stirring occasionally; remove from the heat. Cover the oatmeal and let stand for 8 minutes, or until the desired consistency. (It will continue to thicken as it stands.) Stir in the brown sugar. Spoon the oatmeal into bowls and top with the oranges, dates, and almonds.

Makes 2 servings
Per serving: 295 calories; 7 g protein; 59 g carbohydrate; 5 g fat; 0 mg cholesterol; 6 g dietary fiber; 156 mg sodium

Number of 5 A Day servings: 1.5

quick cook

Toasting Nuts

Toasted nuts add great flavor and crunch to lots of dishes. Toasting does two things: it brings out the flavor of nuts and crisps them, too. This is especially important when nuts are added to wet ingredients, such as salad greens, citrus fruit, and muffin or cake batter. Spread the nuts in a jelly-roll pan; place in a preheated 350°F oven for 7 to 10 minutes, or until lightly toasted and golden, tossing frequently.

texas breakfast parfait

30 minutes or less

3	medium kiwifruit (see below)
2	medium red grapefruit, sectioned
1	cup honey and oat granola
2	(6-ounce) containers custard-style yogurt, such as vanilla, banana, or strawberry
	Mint sprigs, for garnish

Peel the kiwifruit, cut lengthwise into quarters, then thinly slice. Reserve 8 slices for garnish.

To assemble the parfaits, divide the grapefruit sections among parfait glasses. Spoon about 1 tablespoon yogurt over the grapefruit. Sprinkle with about 2 tablespoons granola then top with another layer of yogurt and one-fourth of the kiwifruit. Continue layering with the remaining yogurt, granola, and grapefruit. Top with the reserved kiwifruit and garnish with the mint.

Makes 4 servings
Per serving: 259 calories; 7.5 g protein; 60 g carbohydrate; 8 g fat; 11 mg cholesterol; 5 g dietary fiber, 100 mg sodium
Number of 5 A Day servings: 1

variation

Substitute about 1 cup diced peaches, nectarines, mango, cantaloupe, or honeydew for the kiwifruit.

fruit basket waffles

1	jar (26 ounces) sliced cling peaches
1	tablespoon cornstarch
¾	teaspoon ground cinnamon
1	banana, sliced
1	tablespoon fresh lemon juice
1	cup red or green seedless grapes
8	slices low-fat low-sodium ham (optional)
8	low-fat waffles, toasted and kept warm

Drain the peaches reserving 1 cup of the syrup. Pour the syrup into a small saucepan; set the peaches aside. Add the cornstarch and cinnamon to the syrup, stirring until blended and smooth. Cook over medium-high heat, stirring constantly, until the mixture thickens and boils.

Brush the banana with the lemon juice to prevent browning. In a large bowl, combine the banana, peaches, and grapes with the syrup mixture. Place a waffle on each plate, top with a ham slice if desired, and some of the fruit mixture.

Makes 8 servings
Per serving: 182 calories; 5 g protein; 39 g carbohydrate; 1 g fat; 3 mg cholesterol; 2 g dietary fiber; 358 mg sodium

Number of 5 A Day servings: 1

tropical breakfast parfait

2	cups chopped fresh pineapple
½	pint raspberries (about 1 cup)
1	cup low-fat vanilla yogurt
1	medium banana, sliced
⅓	cup chopped dates
¼	cup sliced almonds, toasted

In stemmed glasses, layer the pineapple, raspberries, yogurt, banana, and dates. Sprinkle the almonds on top and serve.

Makes 4 servings
Per serving: 179 calories; 4.4 g protein; 39.7 g carbohydrate; 2 g fat; 3 mg cholesterol; 4.9 g dietary fiber; 42 mg sodium

Number of 5 A Day servings: 2

sweet potato pancakes
with apple-walnut topping

6	cups shredded sweet potatoes or yams
¼	cup all-purpose flour
½	teaspoon baking powder
¼	teaspoon ground cinnamon
1	tablespoon honey
1	large egg
2	large egg whites

Apple-Walnut Topping

½	cup firmly packed light brown sugar
⅓	cup chopped walnuts
1	tablespoon orange juice
½	teaspoon ground cinnamon
2	baking apples, such as McIntosh or Cortland, peeled, cored, and thinly sliced

In a large bowl, combine the sweet potatoes, flour, baking powder, cinnamon, honey, egg, and egg whites and stir with a fork until mixed well.

Coat a large nonstick skillet with cooking spray and place over medium heat. Drop the batter by about 2 tablespoonfuls into the hot pan to make several pancakes. Flatten slightly with a spatula until about 3 inches across. Cook the pancakes until golden on both sides. Transfer the pancakes to a warm large plate and keep warm. Repeat with the remaining batter, coating the skillet with cooking spray, as needed.

To make the topping: In a large skillet, stir together the brown sugar, walnuts, orange juice, and cinnamon, Add the apples and cook over medium-high heat, stirring, until the apples are tender and the brown sugar has melted to form a syrup. Serve with the pancakes.

Makes 4 servings (12 pancakes)
Per serving: 383 calories; 8.2 g protein; 75.1 g carbohydrate; 7.7 g fat; 53 mg cholesterol; 9.5 g dietary fiber; 106 mg sodium

Number of 5 A Day servings: 3.5

tomato, garlic, and pesto omelet

½	slice whole-wheat bread
½	teaspoon olive oil
1	clove garlic, minced
3	large egg whites
1	teaspoon water
	Salt (optional)
1	teaspoon margarine or butter
2	tablespoons coarsely grated part-skim mozzarella cheese
1	teaspoon prepared pesto
1	large tomato, coarsely chopped

Preheat the oven to 300°F. Cut the bread into cubes; toss with the oil and garlic in a small bowl. Spread the cubes in a single layer on a baking sheet and toast in the oven for 15 to 25 minutes, or until golden brown, tossing once or twice. Transfer to a plate to cool.

In a small bowl, lightly beat together the egg whites, water, and salt, if desired. In a medium nonstick omelet pan or skillet, melt the margarine over medium-high heat. When it starts to sizzle, pour in the egg whites. Begin stirring the eggs with a fork in a circular motion. When the eggs begin to set and form curds, spread them evenly across the bottom of the pan and reduce the heat to very low. When the top layer of egg is almost set, sprinkle the cheese on top then dot with the pesto. Scatter the tomatoes and croutons over half of the omelet; fold the unfilled omelet half over the filling. Slide the omelet onto a plate and serve.

Makes 1 serving
Per serving: 229 calories; 19 g protein; 18.3 g carbohydrate; 9.7 g fat; 4 mg cholesterol; 3.1 g dietary fiber; 435 mg sodium

Number of 5 A Day servings: 1

appleade

32	ounces apple cider or apple juice
8	ounces orange juice
4	ounces frozen limeade concentrate
4	ounces frozen lemonade concentrate
32	ounces ginger ale or lemon-lime soda, chilled
	Ice cubes, for serving

In a large pitcher, combine the apple cider, orange juice, and limeade and lemonade concentrates. Refrigerate. Just before serving, pour in the ginger ale. Fill tall glasses with ice cubes and add the appleade.

Makes 6 servings
Per serving: 251 calories; 0.5 g protein; 64.1 g carbohydrate; 0.3 g fat; 0 mg cholesterol; 0.4 g dietary fiber; 24 mg sodium

Number of 5 A Day servings: 1

hot spiced cider

64	ounces apple cider
2	tablespoons firmly packed brown sugar
1	teaspoon whole allspice berries
1	teaspoon whole cloves
6	cinnamon sticks

In a large saucepan, combine the apple cider, brown sugar, allspice, and cloves and bring to a boil over high heat. Reduce the heat and simmer for 15 minutes. Pour the cider through a strainer set over large mugs. Place a cinnamon stick in each mug and serve.

Makes 6 servings
Per serving: 71 calories; 0 g protein; 3.5 g carbohydrate; 0 g fat; 0 mg cholesterol; 0.4 g dietary fiber; 7 mg sodium

Number of 5 A Day servings: 1

grapefruit fizz

| 32 | ounces sparkling water or seltzer, chilled |
| 6 | ounces frozen grapefruit juice concentrate, thawed |

In a large pitcher, gently stir together the sparkling water and grapefruit juice concentrate until blended. Pour into glasses and serve.

Makes 4 servings
Per serving: 62 calories; 1 g protein; 15 g carbohydrate; 0 g fat; 0 mg cholesterol; 0 g dietary fiber; 52 mg sodium

Number of 5 A Day servings: 1

wild grape slush

1½	cups seedless grapes
8	ounces orange juice concentrate, thawed, or fruit juice
3	cups crushed ice

In a blender, combine all the ingredients and puree until smooth. Pour into glasses and serve.

Makes 4 servings
Per serving: 175 calories; 0.6 g protein; 45 g carbohydrate; 0.5 g fat; 0 mg cholesterol; 0.9 g dietary fiber; 4 mg sodium

Number of 5 A Day servings: 1.5

quick cook

Watermelon-Lime Slush

Serve this drink at your next backyard barbecue. Cut chilled watermelon into chunks and remove the seeds (or use seedless watermelon). In a blender, puree the watermelon, in batches if necessary, until smooth, then pour into a pitcher. Add superfine sugar and fresh lime juice to taste. Fill tall glasses with ice cubes and add the slush. Garnish each drink with a small, thin watermelon slice and wedge of lime.

tangy fresh orangeade

1	cup fresh lemon juice (about 6 lemons)
¾ to 1	cup sugar
4	cups freshly squeezed orange juice (about 12 oranges)
	Ice cubes, for serving
	Orange and lemon slices, for garnish

In a large pitcher, combine the lemon juice and sugar to taste, stirring until sugar dissolves. Stir in the orange juice. Refrigerate until ready to serve. Fill glasses with ice cubes and add the orangeade. Garnish with orange and lemon slices.

Makes 6 servings
Per serving: 180 calories; 1 g protein; 45 g carbohydrate; less than 1 g fat; 0 mg cholesterol; 0.5 g dietary fiber; 10 mg sodium

Number of 5 A Day servings: 1

northwest pear slush

1	large pear, peeled, cored, and coarsely chopped (about 1 cup)
2	ounces orange juice
2	tablespoons fresh lime juice
1	tablespoon honey
1	cup crushed ice

In a blender, combine all the ingredients and puree until smooth. Pour into chilled glasses and serve.

Makes 2 servings
Per serving: 99 calories; 0.6 g protein; 25.8 g carbohydrate; 0.4 g fat; 0 mg cholesterol; 2 g dietary fiber; 0.9 mg sodium

Number of 5 A Day servings: 1

quick cook

Any-Fruit Smoothie

Serve this luscious (and healthy) drink for breakfast, as an after-school snack, or to satisfy a sweet tooth. For one or two servings, combine 1 cup of cut-up ripe fruit (such as banana, strawberries, peaches, mango, and blueberries), ½ cup fat-free plain yogurt, ½ cup fat-free milk, ½ cup ice cubes, a pinch of sugar, and a little vanilla extract or ground cinnamon. Puree until smooth and pour into tall glasses. Delicious!

strawberry sangria ice

2	pints strawberries, hulled
¼	cup sugar
1	cup dry red wine
2	tablespoons fresh lemon juice
1½	tablespoons frozen orange juice concentrate, thawed
	Sparkling water
	Orange slices and mint sprigs, for garnish

In large bowl, crush one-fourth of the strawberries with the sugar with a fork or potato masher. Add the wine, lemon juice, and orange juice concentrate, stirring until the sugar dissolves; pour into a metal baking pan. Cover and freeze for about 2 hours, or until partially frozen. Stir with a wooden spoon to break up the ice; freeze for about 2 hours longer, or until firm.

To serve, set aside 8 strawberries for garnish. Cut the remaining berries in half. Place spoonfuls of the sangria ice into glasses, dividing it evenly and add the cut strawberries. Fill the glasses with sparkling water and garnish with the reserved whole strawberries, orange slices, and mint sprigs.

Makes 4 servings
Per serving: 173 calories; 2 g protein; 33 g carbohydrate; 1 g fat; 0 mg cholesterol; 3.5 g dietary fiber; 5 mg sodium

Number of 5 A Day servings: 2

triple-fruit smoothie

8	ounces apple-cranberry juice
1½	cups applesauce
1	small banana, sliced
2 to 4	ounces low-fat vanilla-flavored soy or rice milk

In a blender, combine all the ingredients and puree until thick and smooth. Pour into glasses and serve.

Makes 2 servings
Per serving: 208 calories; 1 g protein; 52 g carbohydrate; 0.6 g fat; 0 mg cholesterol; 3 g dietary fiber; 31 mg sodium

Number of 5 A Day servings: 2.5

island shake

1   medium banana
1   mango, peeled and cubed
8   ounces pineapple juice
4   ounces low-fat peach yogurt
½   teaspoon finely grated lemon zest
½   cup ice cubes
     Orange wedges and lime slices,
     for garnish

In a blender or food processor, combine the banana, mango, pineapple juice, yogurt, lemon zest, and ice. Puree until thick and smooth. Pour into glasses and garnish with orange wedges and lime slices.

Makes 3 servings
Per serving: 140 calories; 3 g protein; 33 g carbohydrate; 0 g fat; 2 mg cholesterol; 2.4 g dietary fiber; 25 mg sodium

Number of 5 A Day servings: 1

blueberry fruit shake

2   cups frozen blueberries
1   cup frozen mixed fruit
     (cantaloupe, honeydew, grapes,
     and peaches)
8   ounces milk
1   tablespoon sugar
2   teaspoons vanilla extract

In a blender or food processor, combine the blueberries, mixed fruit, milk, sugar, and vanilla; puree until thick and smooth. Pour into glasses and serve.

Makes 3 servings
Per serving: 187 calories; 4.4 g protein; 41.2 g carbohydrate; 1 g fat; 6.1 mg cholesterol; 4.4 g dietary fiber; 46 mg sodium

Number of 5 A Day servings: 2

rio breakfast shake

2	red grapefruit, plus a thin slice of grapefruit cut in half, for garnish
1	cup peeled and diced mango
1	medium banana, sliced
1	container (8 ounces) fat-free strawberry-banana yogurt
2½	tablespoons honey, or more to taste
½	teaspoon vanilla extract
1	cup crushed ice

Squeeze enough grapefruit juice to equal 1⅓ cups. In a blender, combine the grapefruit juice, mango, banana, yogurt, 2½ tablespoons honey, vanilla, and crushed ice and puree until thick and smooth. Sweeten with additional honey, if desired. Pour into glasses and garnish with the grapefruit slices.

Makes 2 servings
Per serving: 320 calories; 6.5 g protein; 80.7 g carbohydrate; 0 g fat; 0 mg cholesterol; 7 g dietary fiber; 75 mg sodium

Number of 5 A Day servings: 3.5

quick cook

Clean Cooking

Keeping your kitchen clean is the best safeguard against harmful bacteria. Replace the kitchen towel and sponge often. You can also put your sponge in the dishwasher or microwave while damp for one minute. Once a week, sterilize plastic cutting boards and countertops by cleaning with a weak bleach solution or with full-strength white vinegar. And, of course, always wash your hands with warm, soapy water before and after handling food, especially raw fish, meat and poultry, and eggs.

after-school strawberry shake

30 minutes or less

kid-friendly

1	pint strawberries, hulled, plus 3 whole strawberries, for garnish
2	medium bananas, peeled and cut into 1-inch chunks
½	cup fat-free strawberry or plain yogurt
4	ounces orange juice
2	tablespoons honey
3	cups ice cubes

In a blender, combine all the ingredients except 1½ cups of the ice cubes and puree until smooth. Add the remaining ice; blend until smooth. Pour into tall glasses and garnish with whole strawberries.

Makes 3 servings
Per serving: 188 calories; 3 g protein; 46 g carbohydrate; 1 g fat; 1 mg cholesterol; 3 g dietary fiber; 20 mg sodium

Number of 5 A Day servings: 2

quick cook

Hulling Strawberries

Here's a good way to remove strawberry stems without wasting any of the delicious flesh: using the tip of a small knife, cut the stem out by rotating the knife tip around the top of the berry (close to the stem), leaving a small cone-shaped hole.

watermelon-strawberry shake

2 cups seeded and cubed watermelon

1 pint strawberries, hulled, plus 4 whole strawberries, for garnish

1 medium banana, sliced

1 container (8 ounces) fat-free lemon yogurt

In a blender or food processor, combine the watermelon, strawberries, banana, and yogurt and puree until smooth and frothy. Pour into glasses and garnish with whole strawberries.

Makes 4 servings
Per serving: 112 calories; 4 g protein; 25 g carbohydrate; 1 g fat; 1 mg cholesterol; 2 g dietary fiber; 16 mg sodium

Number of 5 A Day servings: 2

appetizers,
salsas,
and
chutneys

asparagus tapas
with red pepper sauce

1	tablespoon olive oil
2	large red bell peppers, coarsely chopped, plus thin strips for garnish
2	cloves garlic, minced
1½	pounds asparagus, trimmed
2	tablespoons raspberry vinegar
1½	tablespoons chopped fresh basil, plus additional for garnish
½	teaspoon salt
	Freshly ground black pepper
1	sourdough or French baguette, sliced
	Parmesan cheese shavings, for garnish

In a large skillet, heat the oil over medium heat. Add the bell peppers and garlic; cook, stirring occasionally, for about 15 minutes, or until the peppers are soft. Remove from the heat and let cool slightly.

Meanwhile, in a large saucepan of boiling salted water, cook the asparagus for 4 to 5 minutes, or until crisp-tender; drain. In a blender or food processor, puree the bell peppers until smooth. Stir in the vinegar, basil, salt, and season to taste with black pepper.

To serve, spoon the red pepper sauce onto a platter and arrange the asparagus on top. Garnish with the bell pepper strips, chopped basil, and Parmesan shavings. Serve with the sliced bread.

Makes 4 servings
Per serving: 135 calories; 5.3 g protein; 21.2 g carbohydrate; 4.8 g fat; 0 mg cholesterol; 5.6 g dietary fiber; 450 mg sodium

Number of 5 A Day servings: 2.5

peanut hummus and fresh veggies

Peanut Hummus

1½	cups dried chickpeas, soaked overnight in enough water to cover by 2 inches
¼	cup fresh lemon juice (about 3 large lemons)
1	teaspoon olive oil
⅓	cup reduced fat creamy peanut butter
	Salt and freshly ground black pepper (optional)

Topping

½	small bunch fresh flat-leaf parsley, finely chopped
½	jalapeño pepper, seeded and finely chopped
1	clove garlic, finely chopped
	Extra-virgin olive oil (optional)
	Salt and freshly ground black pepper
½	cup carrot sticks
½	cup celery sticks

In a large saucepan, put the chickpeas and enough water to cover by 2 inches. Bring to a simmer; cover and cook over medium until very soft. (Test a chickpea by crushing it between your fingers; it should be very mushy.) Drain.

In a food processor, puree the chickpeas, lemon juice, and oil, in batches, until smooth. Add some water if the mixture is too thick; process until smooth. Transfer to a large bowl. Stir in the peanut butter and season with salt and pepper, if desired. Stir in a little water to thin the hummus, if necessary.

To make the topping: In a small bowl, combine the parsley, jalapeño, and garlic. Cover with a little extra virgin olive oil, if desired. Season to taste with salt and pepper, if desired.

Spoon some hummus into a serving dish and sprinkle the topping over. Serve the carrot sticks and celery sticks alongside. (The remaining hummus can be refrigerated in a covered container up to 1 week.)

Makes 8 servings
Per serving: 190 calories; 10.6 g protein; 26.2 g carbohydrate; 5.7 g fat; 14.8 mg cholesterol; 5.3 g dietary fiber; 68 mg sodium

Number of 5 A Day servings: 2.5

breakfasts

top: Dried Fruit and Almond Granola

with Yogurt and Banana, p. 39

bottom: Tomato, Garlic,

and Pesto Omelet, p. 44

breakfasts

opposite: Texas Breakfast Parfait, p. 41

top: Watermelon-Strawberry Shake, p. 53

bottom: After-School Strawberry Shake, p. 52

beverages

beverages

beverages

opposite: Wild Grape Slush, p. 46

top: Strawberry Sangria Ice, p. 49

bottom: Tangy Fresh Orangeade, p. 47

appetizers

opposite, top: Creamy Onion Dip, p. 75

opposite, bottom: Thai-Style Marinated

Mushrooms, p. 58

bottom: Curried Grape Salsa, p. 79

salsas

salsas

opposite: Bartlett Pear and Mango Salsa, p. 81

top: Caribbean Salsa, p. 83

bottom: Texas-Style Citrus Salsa, p. 78

|salsas

soup

top: South of the Border Squash Soup, p. 94

opposite: Strawberry Fruit Salad with Three Dressings, p. 111

fruit salads

fruit salads

opposite, top: Crunchy Apple-Walnut Salad, p. 100

opposite, bottom: Root 'n' Cherry Salad, p. 103

bottom: Confetti Fruit Salad, p. 105

|fruit salads

vegetable salads

top: Citrus Slaw, p. 117

bottom: Confetti Pear and Spinach Salad, p. 120

opposite: Vietnamese Cabbage Salad, p. 118

vegetable salads

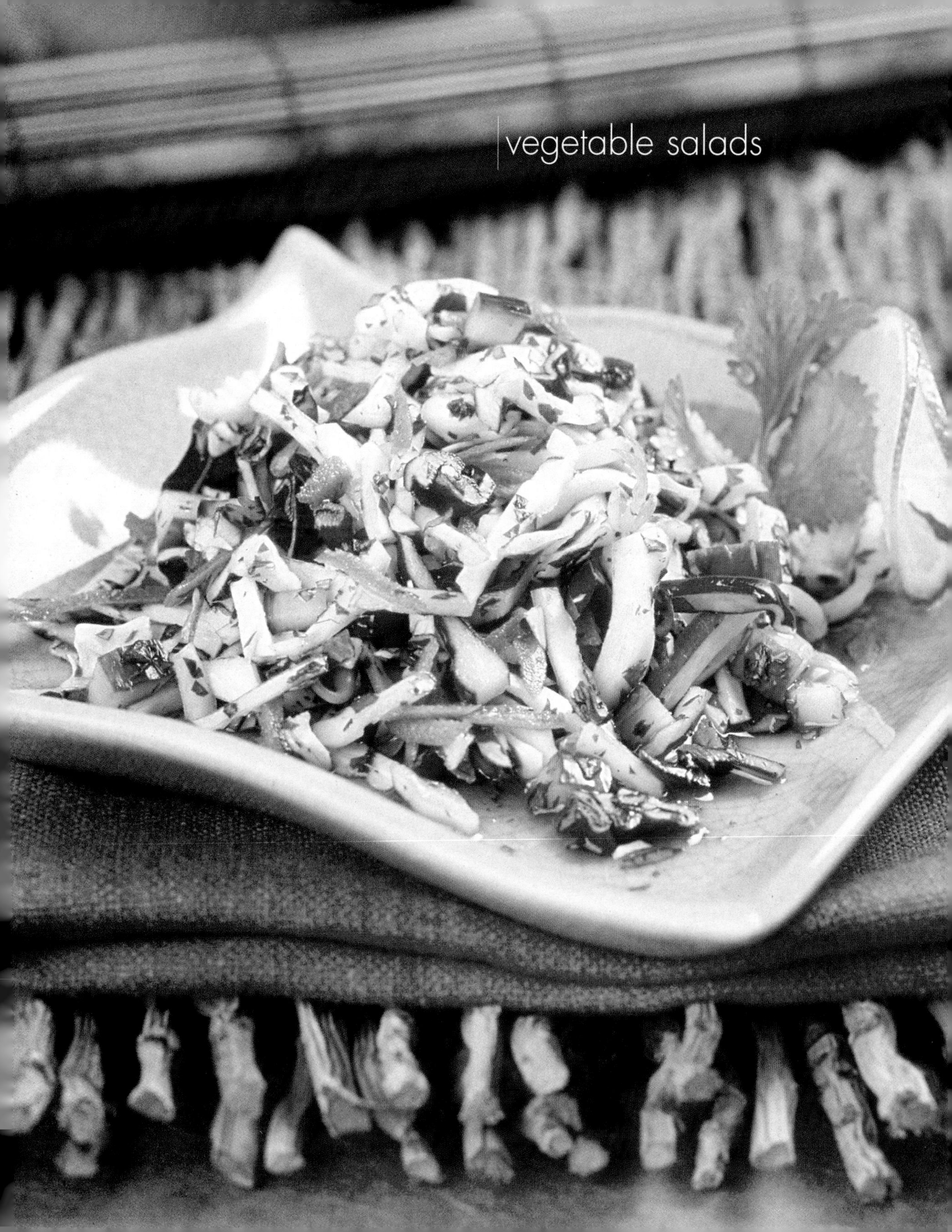

vegetable salads

top: Cool Summer Gazpacho Salad, p. 121

bottom: Penne Salad with Broccoli Rabe, p. 124

creamy onion dip

1	tablespoon olive or vegetable oil
2	large onions, finely chopped (about 2 cups)
1	teaspoon paprika
8	ounces fat-free sour cream Salt and freshly ground black pepper
1	jumbo red onion (about 1 pound), peeled, for serving (optional)

In a medium skillet, heat the oil over medium heat. Add the onions and cook for about 3 minutes, or until barely soft. Stir in the paprika. In a medium bowl, combine the onions and sour cream. Season to taste with salt and pepper. Cover and refrigerate until ready to serve.

To serve the dip in an onion bowl, cut off the top-third of the red onion. Trim the root end to make a flat bottom, leaving enough of the root end intact to hold the onion together. With a melon baller, scoop out the onion center to make a "bowl" for the dip.

Makes 4 servings
Per serving: 46 calories; 2 g protein, 7 g carbohydrate; 2 g fat; 2 mg cholesterol; 0.6 g dietary fiber; 30 mg sodium

Number of 5 A Day servings: 1

quick cook

Roasted Red Peppers

Don't be intimidated by recipes that call for roasted peppers. Here's how to do it: Cut as many bell peppers as you want to roast in half; remove the stems and seeds. Arrange the peppers, cut side down, in a foil-lined broiler pan. Broil, 4 to 6 inches from the heat source, without turning, until the skins are charred and blistered, about 10 minutes. Using tongs, transfer the peppers to a heavy-duty plastic bag and seal. When the peppers are cool enough to handle (about 10 minutes), peel away the skin and discard.

shrimp and vegetable egg rolls

make ahead

1	tablespoon light soy sauce, plus additional for serving
1	teaspoon cornstarch
1	teaspoon sugar
1	teaspoon peanut or light sesame oil
3	scallions, thinly sliced
2	cloves garlic, minced
1	package (6 ounces) frozen mixed Chinese vegetables (pea pods, water chestnuts, and bamboo shoots), thawed and cut into thin strips
1	package (10 ounces) frozen French-cut green beans, thawed
1	package (8 ounces) frozen sliced mushrooms, thawed
1	bag (6 ounces) frozen salad shrimp, thawed slightly
1	tablespoon sesame seeds
1	teaspoon grated fresh ginger
12	egg roll wrappers (see below) Chinese hot mustard, for serving (optional)

Preheat the oven to 425°F. Coat a baking sheet with cooking spray. In a cup, blend the soy sauce, cornstarch, and sugar until smooth; set aside

In a large heavy skillet or wok, heat the oil over medium-high heat until hot but not smoking. Add the scallions and garlic; stir-fry until soft. Add the Chinese vegetables and green beans and stir-fry until tender. Add the mushrooms, shrimp, sesame seeds, and ginger and stir-fry until the shrimp turn pink. Add the cornstarch mixture and stir-fry until the sauce thickens and boils. Reduce the heat and stir-fry for 2 minutes longer. Remove from the heat.

Place the egg roll wrappers on a clean surface with one corner facing you. Spoon ½ cup of the vegetable mixture in the center of each wrapper, then fold in the left and right corners. Moisten the remaining corner and edges with water, then roll tightly to enclose the filling. Arrange the egg rolls on the prepared baking sheet and lightly coat with cooking spray.

Bake, turning once, for 6 to 7 minutes, or until golden brown. Serve with additional soy sauce or hot mustard.

Makes 6 servings (2 egg rolls each)
Per serving: 194 calories; 13.2 g protein; 31.9 g carbohydrate; 2.1 g fat; 50 mg cholesterol; 3.1 g dietary fiber; 435 mg sodium

Number of 5 A Day servings: 1

Cooking Tip

> You can find egg roll wrappers in the produce section of large supermarkets and in Asian markets.

dried fig and fruit salsa

make
ahead

8	ounces dried figs (about 1 cup), chopped
2	medium tomatoes, peeled, seeded, and coarsely chopped
2	medium peaches or nectarines or 1 large mango, peeled and diced
1	small onion, chopped
2	jalapeño peppers, seeded and minced
2	tablespoons chopped fresh mint, cilantro, or basil
2	cloves garlic, minced
2 to 3	teaspoons finely grated lime zest
2	tablespoons fresh lime juice
1	tablespoon balsamic vinegar, (optional)
	Salt and freshly ground black pepper

In a large bowl, combine the figs, tomatoes, peaches, onion, jalapeños, mint, garlic, and lime zest and juice. Stir in the vinegar, if desired, and season to taste with salt and black pepper. Cover and refrigerate for several hours to allow the flavors to blend.

Makes 6 servings
Per serving: 127 calories; 3 g protein; 32 g carbohydrate; 1 g fat; 0 mg cholesterol; 6 g dietary fiber; 7 mg sodium

Number of 5 A Day servings: 1.5

serving suggestion

Serve with chips or vegetable dippers; on broiled or grilled fish, chicken, pork, beef or lamb; over sliced fresh seasonal fruits; on burgers.

texas-style citrus salsa

1	red grapefruit, sectioned and chopped
1	large orange, sectioned and chopped
1	medium tomato, seeded and chopped
1	cup diced green, red, or yellow bell pepper (about 1 large), or a combination
1	jalapeño pepper, seeded and minced
3	tablespoons chopped red onion
1	tablespoon chopped fresh cilantro
1½	teaspoons sugar
¼	teaspoon salt

In a large bowl, combine all the ingredients; toss to mix well. Cover and refrigerate up to several hours. Drain well before serving.

Makes 4 servings
Per serving: 70 calories; 1.5 g protein; 15.6 g carbo-hydrate; 0 g fat; 0 mg cholesterol; 3 g dietary fiber; 125 mg sodium

Number of 5 A Day servings: 1.5

quick cook

Creamy Artichoke Dip

Here's an appetizing low-fat artichoke dip to serve at your next party. In a small bowl, combine ½ cup fat-free sour cream or plain yogurt, ½ cup fat-free mayonnaise, ¼ cup finely chopped fresh parsley, 1 to 2 tea-spoons dried dillweed (optional), 1 small clove garlic, minced, about 2 teaspoons Dijon mustard, and salt and freshly ground pepper to taste. Cover and refrigerate until ready to serve. Makes about 1 cup.

curried grape salsa

1	teaspoon vegetable oil
2	tablespoons chopped red bell pepper
1	teaspoon curry powder
1	cup seedless red grapes, coarsely chopped, plus 4 whole grapes, for garnish
1	cup seedless green grapes, coarsely chopped
2	tablespoons mango chutney
½	teaspoon finely grated fresh ginger
½	teaspoon salt
	Rosemary sprigs, for garnish

In a medium skillet, heat the oil over medium heat. Add the bell pepper and curry powder. Cook, stirring, for about 2 minutes, or just until the mixture is fragrant. Transfer to a medium bowl and add the remaining ingredients. Toss to mix well. Cover and refrigerate for at least 1 hour to allow the flavors to blend. Drain well before serving. Garnish with whole grapes and rosemary sprigs.

Makes 4 servings (1½ cups)
Per serving: 91 calories; 0.7 g protein; 18.7 g carbohydrate; 2.5 g fat; 0 mg cholesterol; 1.2 g dietary fiber; 79 mg sodium

Number of 5 A Day servings: 1

serving suggestion

Serve with crisp pita bread: Split pita bread into two rounds and cut each round into 8 triangles. Brush on the rough side of triangles with oil. Bake at 375°F about 6 to 8 minutes, or until crisp.

kiwifruit-mango salsa

3	medium kiwifruit
¾	cup peeled and chopped mango
1	tablespoon minced green chile peppers, fresh or canned
2	tablespoons fresh lime juice
1½	teaspoons honey
3	tablespoons chopped fresh cilantro
	Pinch of salt
	Tortilla chips, for serving

Peel the kiwifruit, cut lengthwise into quarters, then slice. Put the kiwifruit into a medium bowl and add all the remaining ingredients except the tortilla chips. Mix gently. Serve with tortilla chips.

Makes 3 servings
Per serving: 88 calories; 1.1 g protein; 22.5 g carbohydrate; 0.4 g fat; 0 mg cholesterol; 3.6 g dietary fiber; 25 mg sodium

Number of 5 A Day servings: 1

Cooking Tip

As an alternative, substitute ½ cup (approximately 12) diced dried figs for the mango.

quick cook

Cutting Mango

Mangoes can be a challenge to cut. But they're so delicious and good for you, don't be daunted. Follow this easy technique. Hold the mango in your hand, so that it lies flat in your palm. With a sharp knife, slice the skin in thin strips off the top half. Then cut off all the flesh above the large flat seed. Flip the mango over and repeat the process. Using the tip of the knife, pare away any fruit left clinging to the seed. Chop or slice the mango as needed.

bartlett pear and mango salsa

2	firm-ripe medium Bartlett pears, peeled, cored, and cut into small chunks
½	large mango, peeled and cut into ¼-inch dice
⅓	cup finely chopped yellow bell pepper
⅓	cup finely chopped red bell pepper
¼	cup finely chopped red onion
1	small jalapeño pepper, seeded and minced
3	tablespoons chopped fresh cilantro
3	tablespoons olive oil
2	tablespoons fresh lime juice
¼	teaspoon salt

In a medium bowl, mix together the pears, mango, bell peppers, onion, jalapeño, cilantro, oil, lime juice, and salt. Cover and refrigerate for at least 30 minutes or up to 3 hours.

Makes 6 servings
Per serving: 67 calories; 1 g protein; 14 g carbohydrate; 2 g fat; 0 mg cholesterol; 2 g dietary fiber; 99 mg sodium
Number of 5 A Day servings: 1

quick cook

White Bean and Garlic Spread

Here is a tasty, versatile spread that takes only minutes to make. Spread on toasted or grilled slices of Italian bread and drizzle with a little fruity olive oil for the perfect hors d'oeuvre. The puree also makes a great side dish for grilled or broiled chicken or salmon, especially when topped with chopped tomatoes and basil.

Rinse and drain a 15- to 19-ounce can of cannellini (white kidney) beans and put into a food processor along with a small garlic clove or roasted garlic and pulse to form a rough puree (or mash in a small bowl). Transfer the puree to a bowl, add a little olive oil, and season with salt (optional) and freshly ground pepper. The puree can be stored in the refrigerator in a covered container for up to one week, but serve at room temperature.

chunky fresh tomato salsa

In a food processor, combine the onion, bell pepper, and parsley leaves and process for 10 seconds, scraping down the sides of the bowl. Process until the mixture is finely chopped.

1	small red onion, coarsely chopped
1	medium green bell pepper, coarsely chopped
1	small bunch fresh parsley, stems removed
2	large tomatoes
3	tablespoons red wine vinegar
1	tablespoon fresh lemon juice
1	teaspoon ground cumin or cumin seeds
	Salt and freshly ground black pepper (optional)

Cut the tomatoes crosswise in half and squeeze out most of the juice and seeds. Chop the tomatoes coarsely, then add to the vegetables in the processor. Pulse several times to make a coarse puree that contains little bits of onion and tomato. Transfer the mixture to a serving bowl and stir in the vinegar and lemon juice.

In a small skillet, toast the cumin over low heat, stirring, for 2 to 3 minutes, or just until the cumin starts to smoke. Stir into the salsa and season with salt and black pepper, if desired. Cover and refrigerate until ready to serve. (Can be kept in the refrigerator up to 1 week.)

Makes 6 servings
Per serving: 28 calories; 1 g protein; 6.1 g carbohydrate; 0.4 g fat; 0 mg cholesterol; 1.5 g dietary fiber; 8 mg sodium

Number of 5 A Day servings: 1

Cooking Tip

For a hotter version, substitute 1 seeded fresh jalapeño pepper for the green bell pepper.

caribbean salsa

2	cups seeded and chopped watermelon
1	cup chopped fresh pineapple
1	large onion, chopped (about 1 cup)
¼	cup chopped fresh cilantro
2	ounces orange juice
1	tablespoon chopped jalapeño pepper, or more to taste

In a large bowl, combine all the ingredients and mix well. Cover and refrigerate for at least 1 hour to allow the flavors to blend.

Makes 8 servings
Per serving: 34 calories; 1 g protein; 8 g carbohydrate; 0 g fat; 0 mg cholesterol; 1 g dietary fiber; 3 mg sodium

Number of 5 A Day servings: 1

quick cook

Provençal-Stuffed Tomatoes

Here's a solution for a bumper crop of tomatoes. For every two servings you need one large tomato cut crosswise in half. Gently squeeze out the seeds and juice. Set the tomatoes flat side up in an oiled shallow baking pan and season lightly with salt (optional) and freshly ground black pepper. In a bowl, combine equal amounts of fresh bread crumbs and freshly grated Parmesan cheese. Mix in a bit of chopped parsley (for color), as well as a little minced garlic, salt (optional), and freshly ground black pepper. Top each tomato with about ¼ cup of the crumb mixture, making sure to fill in all the spaces. Drizzle the tomatoes with a little olive oil and bake at 375°F until just beginning to soften, about 25 minutes. Serve hot, warm, or at room temperature.

apple–dried plum chutney

make ahead

½	tablespoon olive oil
1	medium onion, coarsely chopped
½	cup cider vinegar
¼	cup water
1	cup firmly packed light brown sugar
2½	medium apples or pears, or a combination, peeled, cored, and cubed (about 5 cups)
2	cups pitted dried plums
2	tablespoons finely chopped fresh ginger
1	large clove garlic, finely chopped Finely grated zest of 1 lemon
1	cinnamon stick
½	teaspoon salt

In a large Dutch oven or saucepot, heat the oil over medium-high heat. Add the onions and cook, stirring, for 5 to 7 minutes, or until soft. Add the vinegar and water, then stir in the sugar until well mixed. Add all the remaining ingredients and bring to a boil, stirring occasionally. Reduce the heat and simmer, covered, for 20 to 25 minutes, or until the apples are tender, stirring occasionally. Remove from the heat; uncover and cool for 20 minutes.

Spoon into hot sterilized canning jars with lids for gift-giving. (Can be stored in the refrigerator up to 1 month. Remove the cinnamon sticks before serving.)

Makes 4 cups (eight ½-cup servings)
Per serving: 120 calories; 1 g protein; 29 g carbohydrate; 1 g fat; 0 mg cholesterol; 2 g dietary fiber; 80 mg sodium

Number of 5 A Day servings: 1.5

serving suggestion

Serve with baked ham, roasted pork, or smoked turkey.

spicy cherry chutney

make ahead

1	pound sweet cherries, pits and stems removed
¾	cup firmly packed brown sugar
1	medium onion, chopped (about ½ cup)
⅓	cup white vinegar
¼	cup water
1	tablespoon minced fresh ginger
1	small clove garlic, minced
1	teaspoon finely grated lemon zest
½	teaspoon salt
⅛	teaspoon crushed red pepper flakes

In a large heavy pot, combine all the ingredients, stirring to mix well. Bring to a boil over medium-high heat. Reduce the heat and simmer, stirring frequently, for about 1 hour, or until the mixture begins to thicken. Cool completely. Transfer to a covered container and refrigerate up to 2 weeks.

Makes 4 servings
Per serving: 247 calories; 1.6 g protein; 61.8 g carbohydrate; 1.1 g fat; 0 mg cholesterol; 3 g dietary fiber; 18 mg sodium

Number of 5 A Day servings: 1

frozen cherry variation

Remove the cherry stems. Bring the frozen cherries and water to a boil. Remove all the pits using a fork. Add the remaining ingredients and proceed as directed above.

serving suggestion

Serve with roasted chicken, turkey, or pork chops.

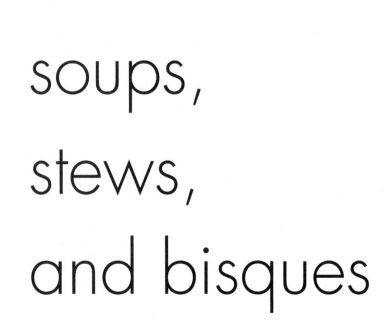

soups,

stews,

and bisques

apple-fennel soup

make ahead

2	medium Golden Delicious apples, peeled, cored, and chopped
2	medium carrots, thinly sliced (about 1 cup)
1	small onion, thinly sliced
½	cup chopped fresh fennel
2	cups water
1	can (14½ ounces) low-sodium chicken broth
½	cup dry white wine
1	bay leaf
¼	teaspoon dried thyme
6	whole black peppercorns
	Low-fat plain yogurt (optional)

In a large pot, combine the apples, carrots, onion, fennel, water, chicken broth, wine, bay leaf, thyme, and peppercorns; bring to a boil over high heat. Reduce the heat and simmer, covered, for 20 minutes.

Pour the soup through a strainer set over a large bowl. Remove the bay leaf. In blender or food processor, puree the vegetable mixture until smooth. Add the soup liquid and pulse until blended. Reheat the soup, if necessary.

To serve, ladle the soup into bowls and top with dollops of yogurt, if desired.

Makes 4 servings
Per serving: 109 calories; 2 g protein; 20 g carbohydrate; 1 g fat; 0 mg cholesterol; 3 g dietary fiber; 42 mg sodium

Number of 5 A Day servings: 1.5

governor's black bean soup

make ahead **kid-friendly**

1	tablespoon olive oil
1	large onion, chopped (about 1 cup)
1	medium carrot, chopped (about ½ cup)
1	medium rib celery, chopped (about ½ cup)
2	cloves garlic, minced
6	cups cooked black beans or about 3 cans (15 to 19 ounces), rinsed and drained
1	can (14½ ounces) whole tomatoes, coarsely chopped
3	cups low-sodium chicken broth
⅓	cup chopped fresh cilantro, plus leaves for garnish
2	tablespoons tomato paste
1	tablespoon fresh lime juice
1	teaspoon ground cumin
⅛	teaspoon cayenne pepper
⅛	teaspoon freshly ground black pepper
½	cup plus 1 tablespoon sour cream

In a large saucepan, heat the oil over medium heat. Add the onion, carrots, celery, and garlic and cook, stirring, for about 10 minutes or until the carrot is soft.

In a food processor, puree the vegetable mixture until smooth. Return the pureed vegetables to the pot; stir in two-thirds of the black beans, the tomatoes plus their juice, the chicken broth, cilantro, tomato paste, lime juice, cumin, cayenne, and black pepper.

In a small bowl, mash the remaining black beans with a fork and add to the soup. Bring to a boil; reduce the heat and simmer for 30 minutes, or until thickened.

To serve, ladle the soup into bowls and top each serving with 1 tablespoon sour cream and a few cilantro leaves.

Makes 9 servings
Per serving: 233 calories; 13 g protein; 39 g carbohydrate; 4 g fat; 9.5 mg cholesterol; 10 g dietary fiber; 423 mg sodium

Number of 5 A Day servings: 2

cold honeydew-lime soup

6½ to 8 pounds honeydew melon (see
    below)

2	teaspoons soybean oil
2	fresh serrano or jalapeño peppers, seeded and minced, or ¼ teaspoon hot red pepper sauce
½	cup fruity white wine, such as Gewürztraminer or Chenin Blanc
⅔	cup fresh lime or lemon juice (about 4 large limes or lemons)
2	tablespoons honey
¼	teaspoon ground white pepper

Cut the melon in half. Scoop out the seeds and discard. With a spoon, scoop out the flesh (you should have 8 to 10 cups). Set aside.

In a small saucepan, heat the oil over medium-high heat. Add the serrano peppers and cook, stirring, for about 3 minutes, or until soft. Add the wine and bring to a boil. (If using hot pepper sauce, omit the oil and stir the hot sauce into the wine.) Remove from the heat.

In a large bowl, combine the melon, wine mixture, lime juice, honey, and white pepper. In a blender or food processor, puree the melon mixture, in batches, until very smooth. Pour into a large bowl and stir until blended. Cover and refrigerate at least 2 hours, or until well chilled.

Makes 8 servings
Per serving: 256 calories; 4 g protein; 60 g carbohydrate; 2 g fat; 0 mg cholesterol; 4 g dietary fiber;
216 mg sodium

Number of 5 A Day servings: 2

serving suggestion

A hollowed-out honeydew shell makes an attractive container for the soup.

chilled nectarine soup

2	pounds nectarines, coarsely chopped
8	ounces apple juice
8	ounces cran-raspberry juice
1	tablespoon balsamic vinegar
½	teaspoon salt
½	teaspoon crushed red pepper flakes
¼	cup lightly packed fresh cilantro leaves

In a blender, combine the nectarines, apple juice, cran-raspberry juice, vinegar, salt, and red pepper flakes and puree until smooth. Add the cilantro and pulse until chopped. Transfer to a large bowl; cover and refrigerate at least 2 hours, or until well chilled.

Makes 5 servings
Per serving: 134.5 calories; 0 g protein; 33 g carbohydrate; 1 g fat; 0 mg cholesterol; 3 g dietary fiber; 244 mg sodium

Number of 5 A Day servings: 2

southwestern pork stew

make ahead

kid-friendly

1¾	pounds pork tenderloin, trimmed and cut into 1-inch pieces
¼	cup all purpose flour
1	large red onion, chopped (about 1 cup)
1¼	pounds sweet potatoes or yams, peeled and cut into 1-inch chunks (see below)
1	package (16 ounces) frozen whole corn kernels, thawed
1	can (10 ounces) chopped tomatoes with green chile peppers
1	can (4 ounces) diced green chile peppers, drained
2	cups low-sodium chicken broth
1	teaspoon chili powder
½	teaspoon ground cumin
	Salt and freshly ground black pepper (optional)

In a medium bowl, toss the pork with the flour until coated, shaking off the excess.

Coat a large pot with cooking spray and place over medium heat. Add the pork and cook, in batches, for 5 to 7 minutes, or until browned on all sides and no longer pink. Add the onion and cook for about 5 minutes, or until soft. Add the sweet potatoes, corn, tomatoes, green chile peppers, chicken broth, chili powder, and cumin. Bring to a boil. Reduce the heat and simmer for about 45 minutes, or until the potatoes and pork are tender. If stew gets too thick, stir in a little chicken broth or water.

Season with salt and pepper, if desired.

Makes 8 servings
Per serving: 297 calories; 26.1 g protein; 39.4 g carbohydrate; 4.1 g fat; 65 mg cholesterol; 5.2 g dietary fiber; 345 mg sodium

Number of 5 A Day servings: 1.5

Cooking Tip

Two cans (29 ounces each) sweet potatoes or yams, drained and cut into chunks can be substituted for the fresh potatoes. Add them to the stew at the end of the cooking to heat through.

two-potato bisque

1	large sweet potato or yam, peeled and cut into 1-inch cubes
1	large baking potato, peeled and cut into 1-inch cubes
1	large onion, chopped (about 1 cup)
2	cloves garlic, minced
1	bay leaf
1	teaspoon dried thyme
⅛	teaspoon cayenne pepper
2	cups low-sodium chicken broth
8	ounces low-fat buttermilk
8	ounces fat-free milk
2	tablespoons fresh lime juice
	Salt and freshly ground black pepper
3	tablespoons chopped fresh cilantro (optional)

In a large saucepot, combine the sweet potato, baking potato, onion, garlic, bay leaf, thyme, cayenne, and chicken broth. Bring to a boil. Reduce the heat and simmer, covered, for 15 minutes, or until the potatoes are tender.

In a food processor, puree the potato mixture until smooth. Return to the pot and stir in the buttermilk, milk, and lime juice. Season to taste with salt and pepper. Cook over low heat until heated through; do not boil.

To serve, ladle the soup into bowls and sprinkle with the cilantro, if desired.

Makes 6 servings
Per serving: 99 calories 4.7 g protein; 8.9 g carbohydrate; 0.6 g fat; 2 mg cholesterol; 1.8 g dietary fiber; 257 mg sodium

Number of 5 A Day servings: 1

south of the border squash soup

2	tablespoons margarine or butter
2	medium onions, chopped
1	medium carrot, chopped (about ½ cup)
2	cloves garlic, chopped
1	butternut squash (about 2½ pounds), peeled, seeded, and cubed
2	jalapeño peppers, seeded and chopped
5	cups low-sodium chicken broth
1	cup tomato puree
	Salt and freshly ground black pepper
	Lime wedges, for serving

In a large saucepan, melt the margarine over medium heat. Add the onions, carrot, and garlic and cook for 3 minutes. Cover the pan. Reduce the heat to low and cook for 3 or 4 minutes longer, or until the vegetables are very soft. Stir in the butternut squash, jalapeños, chicken broth, and tomato puree. Bring to a simmer; cook for 30 minutes.

Mash the squash to a chunky puree with a potato masher or the back of a spoon. Season to taste with salt and black pepper. Ladle into bowls and pass lime wedges separately to be squeezed into each bowl of soup.

Makes 8 servings
Per serving: 126 calories; 4 g protein; 23 g carbohydrate; 4 g fat; 8 mg cholesterol; 5 g dietary fiber; 207 mg sodium

Number of 5 A Day servings: 2

quick cook

Roasted Garlic

Roasted garlic is great for spreading on thin slices of toasted bread. You can also toss it with cooked vegetables.

Slip off the papery skins from one or more whole heads of garlic; cut off the top one-fourth of the heads and discard. Place them, cut side up, on a sheet of heavy-duty aluminum foil; drizzle with a little olive oil and sprinkle with salt (optional) and freshly ground black pepper. Loosely enclose the garlic in the foil and bake at 350°F, until the garlic is soft, about 1 hour. Let cool, then squeeze the soft garlic from each clove into a dish and mash with a fork. The roasted garlic can be stored in the refrigerator in a covered container for up to 5 days.

sweet potato–pear soup

2	teaspoons vegetable oil
1	large onion, chopped (about 1 cup)
1	medium rib celery, sliced (about ½ cup)
3	medium sweet potatoes, peeled and cubed (about 3 cups)
2	ripe medium pears, peeled and cubed (about 2 cups), plus 1 small ripe pear for garnish
4	cups low-sodium chicken broth
½	cup dry vermouth
1	cinnamon stick
1	teaspoon finely grated orange zest
½	teaspoon dried thyme
¼	teaspoon ground nutmeg
¼	teaspoon salt
¼	teaspoon freshly ground black pepper
1	container (8 ounces) low-fat plain yogurt (optional)
	Finely chopped fresh parsley, for garnish

In a large saucepan, heat the oil over medium heat. Add the onion and celery and cook for about 10 minutes, or until soft but not browned. Add the sweet potatoes, pears, chicken broth, vermouth, cinnamon stick, orange zest, and thyme. Bring to a boil; reduce the heat and simmer, covered, for 35 to 45 minutes, or until the sweet potatoes are tender. Remove the cinnamon stick.

In a food processor or blender, puree the vegetable mixture, in batches, until smooth. Return the puree to the saucepan and stir in the nutmeg, salt, and pepper. Cook over medium heat until heated through.

To serve, halve, core, and cut the pear into 6 wedges. Cut each wedge to form a fan. Ladle the soup into bowls and top with a dollop of yogurt, if desired. Garnish each serving with a pear fan and sprinkle with parsley.

Makes 6 servings
Per serving: 189 calories; 4 g protein; 34 g carbohydrate; 4 g fat; 3 mg cholesterol; 5 g dietary fiber; 192 mg sodium

Number of 5 A Day servings: 2

blackened tomato soup

make ahead

kid-friendly

2	tablespoons olive oil
2	pounds tomatoes, cut crossswise in half
1	large red onion, finely chopped (about 1 cup)
3	large cloves garlic, minced
2	small zucchini, diced
1	medium green bell pepper, diced
1	package (10 ounces) frozen whole kernel corn, thawed
1	teaspoon minced jalapeño pepper
1	tablespoon chopped fresh thyme or 1 teaspoon dried
1	teaspoon paprika
3	cups low-sodium chicken broth Salt and freshly ground black pepper
1	container (8 ounces) low-fat plain yogurt
1	large tomato, seeded and diced
1	tablespoon olive oil
1	tablespoon balsamic vinegar Salt and freshly ground black pepper

Preheat the broiler. Brush 1 tablespoon of the oil over the cut sides of the tomatoes. Place the tomatoes, cut side down, in a foil-lined broiler pan. Broil, 4 to 6 inches from the heat source, for about 15 minutes, or until the skin begins to blacken, turning them with tongs, as needed.

When the tomatoes are cool enough to handle, slip off most of the blackened skins. Pass the tomatoes through a food mill set over a bowl. Set aside.

In a medium saucepan, heat the remaining oil over medium heat. Add the onion and one-third of the garlic; cook for about 5 minutes, or until soft. Add the zucchini and bell pepper and cook for 2 to 3 minutes. Stir in the corn, jalapeño, thyme, paprika, and tomatoes; cook for 2 to 3 minutes longer. Add the chicken broth and season to taste with salt and black pepper. Bring to a boil; reduce the heat and simmer, partially covered, for 45 minutes.

Meanwhile, in a small bowl, combine the yogurt and remaining garlic. Set aside in the refrigerator. In a small bowl, combine the tomato, oil, and vinegar. Season to taste with salt and black pepper.

To serve, ladle the soup into bowls, swirl some of the yogurt into each serving, and top with the tomato mixture.

Makes 6 servings
Per serving: 197 calories; 8.3 g protein; 29.7 g carbohydrate; 7.3 g fat; 4 mg cholesterol; 5.1 g dietary fiber; 107 mg sodium

Number of 5 A Day servings: 3

watermelon gazpacho

6	cups seeded and cubed watermelon
2	medium Golden Delicious apples, cored and chopped (about 1½ cups)
1	medium onion, finely chopped (about ½ cup)
½	cup finely chopped green bell pepper
1	teaspoon dried basil
½	teaspoon salt
¼	teaspoon coarsely ground black pepper
¼	teaspoon chili powder
1	tablespoon cider vinegar

In a blender, puree the watermelon until smooth; pour into a large bowl. Stir in the remaining ingredients. Cover and refrigerate at least 2 hours, or until well chilled.

Makes 4 servings
Per serving: 114 calories; 2 g protein; 27 g carbohydrate; 1 g fat; 0 mg cholesterol; 3 g dietary fiber; 298 mg sodium

Number of 5 A Day servings: 4

fruit

salads

crunchy apple-walnut salad

Apple–Walnut Oil Dressing

¼	cup walnut or olive oil
4	tablespoons apple juice
2	tablespoons balsamic vinegar
½	teaspoon Dijon mustard
¼	teaspoon salt
¼	teaspoon freshly ground black pepper

Salad

5	ounces mixed salad greens (about 6 cups)
4	medium Braeburn or Fuji apples, cored and cut into chunks
2	tablespoons chopped walnuts
1	tablespoon freshly grated Parmesan cheese

To make the dressing: In a small jar with tight-fitting lid, combine all the dressing ingredients and shake well.

To make the salad: In a large salad bowl, combine the salad greens, apples, and walnuts. Drizzle the dressing over the salad and toss until evenly coated. Sprinkle with the Parmesan and toss thoroughly.

Makes 6 servings
Per serving: 113 calories; 1.9 g protein; 18.3 g carbohydrate; 4.6 g fat; 0.8 mg cholesterol; 3.6 g dietary fiber; 46 mg sodium

Number of 5 A Day servings: 1

cherry-couscous salad

Salad

1½	cups vegetable broth or water
1½	cups couscous
2	cups pitted sweet cherries (about 1¼ pounds)
1	can (15 to 19 ounces) black beans, rinsed and drained
1	can (11 ounces) whole kernel corn, drained
3	scallions, chopped (about ½ cup)
½	cup chopped fresh parsley
½	cup chopped green bell pepper

Fresh Lime Dressing

½	teaspoon finely grated lime zest
¼	cup fresh lime juice (about 2 limes)
3	tablespoons olive oil
1	teaspoon sugar
½	teaspoon salt (optional)
¼	teaspoon dried oregano, crushed
¼	teaspoon chili powder

In a medium saucepan, bring the vegetable broth to a boil over medium-high heat. Stir in the couscous; cover and remove from the heat. Let stand for 5 minutes, then fluff with a fork. Transfer the couscous to a serving bowl and stir in the cherries, black beans, corn, scallions, parsley, and bell pepper.

To make the dressing: In a small bowl, whisk together all the dressing ingredients until well blended. Drizzle the dressing over the couscous mixture and toss until evenly coated. Serve warm or at room temperature.

Makes 8 servings
Per serving: 281 calories; 9.1 g protein; 49.2 g carbohydrate; 6.6 g fat; 0 mg cholesterol; 7 g dietary fiber; 267 mg sodium

Number of 5 A Day servings: 1.5

quick cook

Zest It Right

Recipes often call for the finely grated zest of lemon, orange, lime, or grapefruit. Citrus peel is made up of two parts: the colorful, flavorful outer layer known as the zest and the white layer underneath called the pith. When grating zest, you want to avoid the pith, which is bitter. To grate, use the fine holes of a box grater or the newest zester on the market called The Microplane Greater Zester, available in cookware stores and in catalogues—they do a terrific job.

northwest cherry and tropical fruit salad

1	large sweet onion, chopped (about 1 cup)
2	tablespoons pineapple juice
1	tablespoon cider vinegar
1	tablespoon honey (optional)
¼	cup chopped fresh basil or 1 tablespoon dried
½	teaspoon salt
⅛	teaspoon ground black pepper
1	large mango, peeled and sliced
12	ounces sweet cherries, pitted and halved (about 1 cup)
1	cup Rainier cherries, pitted and halved
8	fresh pineapple spears

Heat a large nonstick skillet over medium-high heat. Add the onion, pineapple juice, and vinegar; stir-fry for about 4 minutes, or until the onions are soft. Stir in the honey, basil, salt, and pepper. Remove from the heat and let cool.

In a 9 × 13 inch baking dish, place the mango in the middle of the dish, and the cherries and pineapple at either end. Spoon the onion mixture over the fruit and marinate at room temperature for about 1 hour. Serve at room temperature or refrigerate and serve cold.

Makes 4 servings
Per serving: 163 calories; 2.2 g protein; 40 g carbohydrate; 1.5 g fat; 0 mg cholesterol; 4.5 g dietary fiber; 273 mg sodium

Number of 5 A Day servings: 3

root 'n' cherry salad

1	cup carrot matchstick strips
1	cup turnip matchstick strips
1	cup rutabaga matchstick strips
1	cup jicama matchstick strips
½	cup thinly sliced sweet onion
3	tablespoons white wine vinegar
1	tablespoon vegetable oil
1	tablespoon sugar
1	small clove garlic, minced
1	teaspoon salt
⅛	teaspoon hot red pepper sauce
2	cups pitted sweet cherries (about 1¼ pounds)
	Lettuce leaves

In a large bowl, combine all ingredients except the cherries and lettuce and toss until well-mixed. Cover and refrigerate for at least 1 or up to 4 hours. Just before serving, toss in the cherries. Serve on a lettuce-lined plate.

Makes 8 servings
Per serving: 102 calories; 1.8 g protein; 19.2 g carbohydrate; 2.8 g fat; 0 mg cholesterol; 2.6 g dietary fiber; 385 mg sodium

Number of 5 A Day servings: 1.5

serving suggestion

Serve with barbecued chicken or ribs.

tropical fruit ambrosia

1	jar (26 ounces) mixed tropical fruit, drained
1	large banana, sliced
1	cup low-fat vanilla yogurt
¼	teaspoon finely grated lime zest
2	tablespoons fresh lime juice
¼	cup flaked coconut
	Lettuce leaves

In a large bowl, combine the tropical fruit and banana.

In a small bowl, stir together the yogurt and lime zest and juice until blended. Spoon over the fruit and toss until evenly coated. Sprinkle with the coconut. Line a serving bowl with lettuce leaves and spoon in the salad. Sprinkle with the coconut and serve.

Makes 6 servings
Per serving: 150 calories; 2 g protein; 33 g carbohydrate; 2 g fat; 3 mg cholesterol; 2 g dietary fiber; 40 mg sodium

Number of 5 A Day servings: 1

 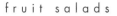

citrus salad
with raspberry-vanilla sauce

make ahead

kid-friendly

Raspberry-Vanilla Sauce

1	package (12 ounces) frozen sweetened raspberries, thawed
2	tablespoons sugar
1	tablespoon cornstarch
⅛	teaspoon ground mace
2	teaspoons vanilla extract

Salad

4	red or white grapefruit, or a combination, sectioned
7	oranges, sectioned
	Mint sprigs, for garnish

To make the sauce: Press the raspberries through a strainer set over a small bowl; discard the seeds. Measure the raspberry puree and add enough water to equal 1¼ cups.

In a small saucepan, mix together the raspberry puree, sugar, cornstarch, and mace until blended. Cook over medium heat, stirring, for about 4 minutes, or until the sauce thickens and boils. Cook for 2 minutes longer. Remove from the heat and stir in the vanilla. Transfer to a covered container and refrigerate for about 2 hours, or until cold.

Arrange the grapefruit and orange sections on a platter. Cover and chill up to several hours.

To serve, drizzle the raspberry sauce over the fruit. Garnish with mint sprigs.

Makes 8 servings
Per serving: 158 calories; 2 g protein; 40 g carbohydrate; 0 g fat; 0 mg cholesterol; 7 g dietary fiber; 1 mg sodium

Number of 5 A Day servings: 2

quick cook

Sectioning Citrus Fruit

With a small knife, slice off the blossom and stem ends of the fruit. Cut away the peel (including all the white pith), using a sawing motion and following the shape of the fruit. To remove the individual sections, cut along the side of each membrane and let each section and its juice fall into a bowl.

Cooking Tip

To quickly chill the raspberry sauce, transfer the sauce to a small bowl and set into a medium bowl of ice water. Stir occasionally until cold.

confetti fruit salad

30 minutes or less

make ahead

kid-friendly

3	oranges, peeled and cut into bite-size pieces
1	medium apple, unpeeled, cut into bite-size pieces
1	medium rib celery, sliced (about ½ cup)
¼	cup raisins
2	tablespoons firmly packed brown sugar
	Finely grated zest and juice of ½ lemon
2	tablespoons coarsely chopped walnuts

In a large salad bowl, combine all the ingredients except the nuts. Cover and refrigerate up to 2 hours. Just before serving, sprinkle the nuts on top.

Makes 4 servings
Per serving: 149 calories; 2 g protein; 33 g carbohydrate; 3 g fat; 0 mg cholesterol; 3 g dietary fiber; 20 mg sodium

Number of 5 A Day servings: 1

quick cook

To Ripen or Not to Ripen?

Some fruits should be eaten the moment you get them home from the store and other fruits need time to ripen. Apples, cherries, lemons, limes, oranges, pomegranates, and rhubarb are fully ripe when purchased, so they can be enjoyed immediately. Other fruits, including apricots, bananas, kiwifruit, mangos, melons, nectarines, papayas, peaches, pears, persimmons, and plums, may require further ripening. Refrigerate all fruits, however, as soon as they are ripe to prevent overripening. Do not store tomatoes in the refrigerator.

honey dijon and pear salad

Lettuce leaves

1   jar (26 ounces) sliced pears, drained

5   ounces alfalfa sprouts or shredded iceberg or romaine lettuce (about 2 cups lightly packed)

1   medium yellow bell pepper, cut into 1-inch pieces

1   medium red bell pepper, cut into 1-inch pieces

1   cup fat-free honey Dijon salad dressing

½   cup chopped walnuts

Line a platter with lettuce leaves and arrange the pears around the edge of the lettuce. Mound the sprouts in center, then place the yellow and red peppers around the pears. Drizzle the dressing over the salad and sprinkle with the nuts.

Makes 7 servings
Per serving: 172 calories; 2.4 g protein; 31 g carbohydrate; 5.3 g fat; 0 mg cholesterol; 3 g dietary fiber; 179 mg sodium

Number of 5 A Day servings: 2

greens with pineapple, apple, and feta

Balsamic-Mustard Vinaigrette

3	tablespoons balsamic vinegar
3	tablespoons water
2	tablespoons honey mustard
1	clove garlic, minced
	Salt and freshly ground black pepper (optional)

Salad

6	cups torn Boston lettuce leaves (about 1 head)
1½	cups pineapple chunks
2	medium Red Delicious apples, cored and thinly sliced
1	small red onion, thinly sliced
3	tablespoons crumbled feta cheese

To make the vinaigrette: In a small bowl whisk together the vinegar, water, mustard, and garlic; season with salt and pepper, if desired.

In a large salad bowl, toss the remaining ingredients. Drizzle the vinaigrette on top and toss gently until evenly coated.

Makes 4 servings
Per serving: 114 calories; 2.8 g protein; 22.7 g carbohydrate; 2.5 g fat; 6.3 mg cholesterol; 4.3 g dietary fiber; 185 mg sodium

Number of 5 A Day servings: 3

quick cook

Creative Core Remover

A melon baller is the perfect tool for neatly and easily removing the cores from apples and pears. Simply cut the fruit in half and scoop out the core.

tropical fruit
with lime dressing

¼	cup honey
2	tablespoons fresh lime juice
6	ounces pitted dried plums (about 1 cup)
1	cup canned or fresh pineapple chunks
3	kiwifruit, peeled and cut into chunks
½	papaya or mango, peeled and cut into chunks
1	large banana or Asian pear, cut into chunks
1	cup seedless red grapes
¼ to ⅓	cup chopped cashews or macadamia nuts (optional)
2	tablespoons chopped crystallized ginger

To make the dressing: In a cup, stir together the honey and lime juice until blended.

In a large bowl, combine the dried plums, pineapple, kiwifruit, papaya, banana and grapes. Drizzle the dressing over the fruit. Toss gently until evenly coated. Serve or cover and refrigerate up to 1 hour. Sprinkle with the nuts if using, and the ginger just before serving.

Makes 4 servings
Per serving: 337 calories; 2.6 g protein; 87.2 g carbohydrate; 0.9 g fat; 0 mg cholesterol; 7 g dietary fiber; 19 mg sodium

Number of 5 A Day servings: 3.5

Cooking Tip

Cut all the fruit into uniform pieces (about ¾ inch) to match the size of the dried plums. Peaches, nectarines, or cantaloupe can be substituted for the papaya or mango.

california fruit salad

30 minutes or less

Dressing

1	tablespoon olive oil
2	tablespoons raspberry vinegar
1	tablespoon chopped walnuts, toasted
3	tablespoons orange juice
1	teaspoon finely grated lime zest
1	tablespoon fresh lime juice
1	tablespoon chopped fresh basil
½	teaspoon dry mustard
¼	teaspoon salt
¼	teaspoon freshly ground black pepper

Salad

1	ripe avocado
8	ounces mixed baby salad greens (about 10 cups)
3	kiwifruit, peeled, cut lengthwise in half, and sliced
2	red or pink grapefruit, sectioned
1	pint strawberries, hulled and sliced (about 2 cups)

To make the dressing: In a small bowl, whisk together all the ingredients until blended.

To make the salad: Cut half of the avocado into 8 wedges and set aside for garnish. Cut the remaining half into cubes. In a large salad bowl, combine all the salad ingredients. Drizzle the dressing over the salad and toss until evenly coated. Arrange the avocado slices on top and serve.

Makes 10 servings
Per serving: 100 calories; 2.2 g protein; 13.4 g carbohydrate; 5.3 g fat; 0 mg cholesterol; 3.9 g dietary fiber; 17 mg sodium

Number of 5 A Day servings: 3

quick cook

Purchasing Fresh Produce

How vegetables and fruit look is the best indication of their freshness and quality. Avoid those with bruises, soft brown spots, or cuts. Artichokes, mushrooms, and citrus fruit should feel heavy for their size. Be sure the tops of leafy greens are crisp and fresh-looking, not wilted or yellowing.

mixed greens
with strawberries and orange

In a large salad bowl, whisk together the vinaigrette ingredients. Add the salad greens and toss until evenly coated. Arrange the strawberries, fennel, orange, and apple on top.

Makes 4 servings
Per serving: 95 calories; 1 g protein; 17 g carbohydrate; 1 g fat; 0 mg cholesterol; 4 g dietary fiber; 74 mg sodium

Number of 5 A Day servings: 2

Vinaigrette Dressing

6	ounces orange juice
2	tablespoons white wine or champagne vinegar
1	teaspoon olive oil
¼	teaspoon freshly ground black pepper
	Pinch of salt

Salad

3	ounces mixed baby salad greens (about 4 cups)
½	cup sliced strawberries
½	cup diced fennel
1	orange, peeled and sliced
1	medium Golden Delicious apple or Bartlett pear, cored and chopped

strawberry fruit salad
with three dressings

2	pounds spinach, tough leaves trimmed (about 8 cups lightly packed)
1	pint strawberries, hulled and halved
4	cups assorted melon chunks
1½	cups orange and grapefruit segments
	Orange-Mint, Strawberry-Ginger, or Balsamic-Pepper Dressing

Line a platter or plates with the spinach. Top with the strawberries, melon, and orange and grapefruit. Serve with your choice of dressing on the side.

Orange-Mint Dressing: In a small bowl, whisk together 1 container (8 ounces) plain fat-free yogurt, 3 tablespoons thawed orange juice concentrate, and 1 teaspoon sugar. Mix in 3 tablespoons chopped fresh mint. Serve immediately, or cover and refrigerate up to 2 days.

Strawberry-Ginger Dressing: In a blender or food processor, puree 1½ cups strawberries until smooth; transfer to a small bowl. Mix in 1½ to 2 tablespoons honey, 1½ tablespoons fresh lime juice, 2 teaspoons grated fresh ginger, and a pinch of salt. Serve or cover and refrigerate up to 2 days.

Balsamic-Pepper Dressing: In a small bowl, whisk together 1 container (8 ounces) strawberry yogurt, 1 tablespoon balsamic vinegar, 1 teaspoon honey, and ½ to 1 teaspoon coarsely ground black pepper. Serve or cover and refrigerate up to 2 days.

Makes 4 servings
Per serving: Strawberry Fruit Salad with Orange-Mint Dressing: 173 calories; 8.5 g protein; 38.4 g carbohydrate; 1.2 g fat; 1 mg cholesterol; 5.6 g dietary fiber; 177 mg sodium
Per serving: Strawberry Fruit Salad with Strawberry Ginger Dressing: 191 calories; 6.3 g protein; 45.2 g carbohydrate; 1.5 g fat; 0 mg cholesterol; 7.2 g dietary fiber; 144 mg sodium
Per serving: Strawberry Fruit Salad with Balsamic Pepper Dressing: 177 calories; 7.8 g protein; 39.2 g carbohydrate; 1.2 g fat; 1 mg cholesterol; 5.6 g dietary fiber; 172 mg sodium

Number of 5 A Day servings: 5.5

vegetable salads

apple-beet salad

30 minutes or less

4	Granny Smith apples, peeled, cored, and sliced
1	can (16 ounces) julienne beets, drained
6	radishes, sliced
2	scallions, diagonally sliced
¼	cup vinegar
¼	cup olive oil
1	teaspoon sugar
¼	teaspoon ground allspice
	Dash of hot red pepper sauce
	Salt and ground black pepper

In a large bowl, combine the apples, beets, radishes, and scallions.

In a small bowl, whisk together the vinegar, oil, sugar, allspice, and hot sauce, if desired. Season to taste with salt and pepper. Drizzle over the apple mixture and toss until evenly coated. Cover and refrigerate at least 1 hour before serving.

Makes 6 servings
Per serving: 187 calories; 1 g protein; 27 g carbohydrate; 9 g fat; 0 mg cholesterol; 5 g dietary fiber; 158 mg sodium

Number of 5 A Day servings: 1.5

mediterranean pasta salad

30 minutes or less

1	cup rotini or bowties
1	can (14¾ ounces) salmon, drained
7	ounces Mediterranean or Greek marinade salad mix
⅔	cup coarsely chopped walnuts (optional)
1	tablespoon freshly grated Parmesan cheese
1	tablespoon fresh lemon juice, plus lemon wedges for garnish

Cook the pasta according to the package directions. Drain. Rinse under cold water and drain.

Break the salmon up into bite-size chunks. In a large salad bowl, combine the salmon, pasta, salad mix, walnuts, and Parmesan. In a cup, mix together the salad mix marinade and the lemon juice. Pour over the salad and toss until evenly coated.

Divide the salad among plates and garnish with lemon wedges.

Makes 4 servings
Per serving: 170 calories; 20.9 g protein; 8.7 g carbohydrate; 5.5 g fat; 34.4 mg cholesterol; 1.2 g dietary fiber; 456 mg sodium

Number of 5 A Day servings: 1

asparagus
and blood orange salad

2	medium shallots, finely chopped
1	tablespoon balsamic vinegar
1	tablespoon sherry vinegar or dry sherry
	Finely grated zest of 1 blood orange
⅓	cup blood orange juice
1	tablespoon extra-virgin olive oil
¼	teaspoon salt
	Freshly ground black pepper
1½	pounds asparagus, trimmed and cut in half
3	blood oranges, peeled and cut into ½-inch-thick slices
	Salt and freshly ground black pepper (optional)
2	tablespoons coarsely chopped walnuts, toasted

In a small bowl, combine the shallots, vinegar, and sherry; let stand for about 20 minutes. Stir in the orange zest and juice. Slowly whisk in the oil until well-blended. Add the salt and season to taste with pepper.

In a large skillet, bring 1 inch of water to a boil over high heat. Add the asparagus and cook for 4 to 5 minutes, or until crisp-tender; drain. Rinse briefly under cold water and drain; transfer to a medium bowl. Drizzle the vinaigrette over the asparagus and toss until evenly coated.

To serve, arrange the orange slices and asparagus on salad plates and season with salt and pepper, if desired. Top each serving with the walnuts.

Makes 4 servings
Per serving: 171 calories; 7 g protein; 25.8 g carbohydrate; 6.5 g fat; 0 mg cholesterol; 5.3 g dietary fiber; 151 mg sodium
Number of 5 A Day servings: 2.5

Cooking Tip

Blood oranges can be found in some large supermarkets and in specialty food stores. If you can't find them, use regular oranges instead.

lemony bean salad

make ahead

Lemon-Mint Dressing

¼	cup fresh lemon juice
1	tablesppon vegetable oil
3	tablespoons chopped fresh mint
1	clove garlic, minced
	Finely grated zest of ½ lemon
2	teaspoons sugar
1	teaspoon Dijon mustard
¼	teaspoon ground white pepper

Salad

1	cup dried chickpeas or small white beans, cooked (see below) or 1 can (15 ounces) beans, rinsed and drained
½	cup chopped red bell pepper or tomato
1	medium onion, chopped
⅓	cup chopped fresh parsley

To make the dressing: In a large bowl, whisk together the lemon juice, oil, mint, garlic, lemon zest, sugar, mustard, and white pepper until blended. Add the beans; cover and refrigerate for about 1 hour, tossing occasionally.

To serve, add the bell pepper, onion, and parsley and toss until well-mixed.

Makes 4 servings
Per serving: 162 calories; 6 g protein; 20 g carbohydrate; 7 g fat; 0 mg cholesterol; 0.9 g dietary fiber; 24 mg sodium

Number of 5 A Day servings: 1

Cooking Tip

To quick-soak and cook dried beans: Combine the beans with enough water to cover by 2 inches in a large saucepan. Bring to a boil over medium-high and cook for 3 minutes. Remove from the heat; cover and set aside for 1 hour. Drain the beans and rinse under cold water.

Drain the beans and return to the pot. Add enough water to cover by 2 inches. Bring to a boil; cover and cook over low heat for 1½ to 2 hours, or until the beans are tender. (The cooking time depends on the type and freshness of the beans.)

citrus slaw

¼	cup bottled fat-free herb vinaigrette
2	ounces frozen orange juice concentrate, thawed
1	pound napa cabbage, shredded (about 4 cups)
2	oranges, sectioned
1	red apple, halved, cored, and sliced
6	ounces pitted dried plums (about 1 cup), quartered
1	medium rib celery, sliced (about ½ cup)
¼	cup sliced scallions
	Freshly ground black pepper (optional)

In a large bowl, whisk together the vinaigrette and orange juice concentrate until blended. Add the cabbage, oranges, apple, dried plums, celery, and scallions, tossing to evenly coat. Season to taste with pepper, if desired.

Makes 6 servings
Per serving: 113 calories; 2 g protein; 28 g carbohydrate; 0 g fat; 0 mg cholesterol; 6 g dietary fiber; 155 mg sodium

Number of 5 A Day servings: 2

quick cook

Farmer's Market Black Bean, Corn, and Tomato Salad

This boldly flavored salad is even better if you use ripe, local tomatoes and freshly picked corn. In a large bowl, combine equal amounts of rinsed and drained canned black beans, whole corn kernels, chopped fresh tomato, and chopped fresh cilantro. Add a little finely chopped red onion, seeded and minced jalapeño pepper, fresh lime juice, salt (optional), and freshly ground black pepper. Let stand for about 1 hour before serving to allow the flavors to blend. For a special presentation, line a bowl with romaine lettuce leaves before spooning in the salad.

vietnamese cabbage salad

¼	cup fresh lime juice
3	tablespoons sugar
¼	cup water
2	tablespoons white or rice vinegar
½	small head green cabbage, chopped (about 5 cups)
2	cups chopped red cabbage
2	medium carrots, coarsely grated (about 1 cup)
1	large cucumber, peeled, seeded, and diced
2	ounces bean sprouts (½ cup)
½	cup lightly packed fresh mint leaves, chopped
½	cup lightly packed fresh cilantro leaves, chopped

In a small bowl, whisk together lime juice, sugar, water, and vinegar until blended.

In a large salad bowl, combine the green and red cabbage, carrots, cucumber, bean sprouts, mint, and cilantro, tossing until mixed. Drizzle the dressing over the salad and toss until evenly coated.

Makes 8 servings
Per serving: 57 calories; 1 g protein; 13 g carbohydrate; 0 g fat; 0 mg cholesterol; 2 g dietary fiber; 21 mg sodium

Number of 5 A Day servings: 1.5

spring salad with dried plums and lemon vinaigrette

30 minutes or less

Lemon Vinaigrette

¼	cup fresh lemon juice
5	teaspoons olive oil
1	tablespoon honey
2	tablespoons chopped fresh basil or 2 teaspoons dried
½	teaspoon finely grated lemon zest
½	teaspoon salt
¼	teaspoon freshly ground black pepper

Spring Salad

6	ounces mixed baby salad greens (about 8 cups)
6	ounces pitted dried plums (1 cup), quartered
1	medium carrot, coarsely grated
1	small Golden Delicious apple, cored and thinly sliced
½	cup walnuts, toasted (optional)

To make the vinaigrette: In a jar with a tight-fitting lid, combine the vinaigrette ingredients and shake until well-blended.

To make the salad: In a large salad bowl, combine the salad green, dried plums, carrot, apple, and walnuts, if desired. Drizzle the dressing over salad and gently toss until evenly coated.

Makes 8 servings
Per serving: 84 calories; 1.3 g protein; 14.8 g carbohydrate; 3 g fat; 0 mg cholesterol; 2.7 g dietary fiber; 20 mg sodium

Number of 5 A Day servings: 1.5

quick cook

Health Salad Sandwiches

When you're tired of serving the same old sandwiches, here's a delicious alternative that boasts under 400 calories and no cholesterol. For each sandwich, toss together 1 grated carrot, ½ cup alfalfa sprouts, and a little fat-free salad dressing and set aside. In a separate bowl, coarsely mash about ½ cup rinsed and drained canned chickpeas and season with garlic powder, ground cumin, salt (optional), freshly ground black pepper, and a squeeze of fresh lemon juice. Spread the bean puree on two slices of multigrain bread. Top one bread slice with sliced tomato, lettuce, arugula, or watercress. Top the other slice with the carrot mixture and invert to make a sandwich.

confetti pear and spinach salad

1	package (10 ounces) fresh spinach, tough stems trimmed
1	can (15 ounces) sliced Bartlett pears in light syrup, drained
½	cup chopped red bell pepper
½	cup coarsely chopped walnuts (optional)
3	slices bacon, cooked crisp and crumbled
¼	cup bottled balsamic vinegar dressing
1	teaspoon finely grated orange zest

In a large salad bowl, combine the spinach, pears, bell pepper, walnuts if desired, and bacon. In a small bowl, whisk together the balsamic dressing and orange zest. Drizzle over the salad and toss until evenly coated.

Makes 6 servings
Per serving: 187 calories; 5 g protein; 17 g carbohydrate; 12 g fat; 3 mg cholesterol; 3 g dietary fiber; 245 mg sodium

Number of 5 A Day servings: 2

quick cook

Tuscan-Style Spinach

This easy dish adds an Italian accent to any dinner. In a large skillet, cook several whole garlic cloves in a splash of olive oil over medium heat until the garlic is soft and golden. Add well-washed, dried, and torn fresh spinach leaves (don't forget to remove the tough stems), and season with salt (optional) and freshly ground black pepper. Cook, stirring, until the spinach is wilted, about 4 minutes. Discard the garlic, if desired.

cool summer gazpacho salad

1	large pineapple
1	large tomato, seeded and chopped
1	small cucumber, seeded and chopped
2	tablespoons chopped onion
1	tablespoon chopped fresh parsley
2	tablespoons red wine vinegar
1	tablespoon vegetable oil
½	teaspoon salt
	Dash of garlic powder

Twist the pineapple crown to separate it from the pineapple. Cut the pineapple lengthwise in half. Stand the pineapple up and slice off the rind and eyes. Cut each pineapple half lengthwise in half. Slice off the core and cut the pineapple into chunks.

In a large bowl, combine the pineapple, tomato, cucumber, onion, and parsley. In a jar with a tight-fitting lid, combine the vinegar, oil, salt, and garlic powder; shake until well-blended. Drizzle the dressing over the salad and toss until evenly coated.

Makes 4 servings
Per serving: 139 calories; 2 g protein; 27 g carbo-hydrate; 3 g fat; 0 mg cholesterol; 2.4 g dietary fiber; 307 mg sodium

Number of 5 A Day servings: 3

quick cook

Tomato and Red Onion Salad

The success of this sprightly salad depends on the ripest tomatoes and freshest herbs you can find. For four servings, thinly slice a small red onion and almost cover with red wine vinegar in a bowl. Let stand for at least 30 minutes or up to several hours, tossing occasionally; drain and reserve the vinegar. Add 3 large tomatoes cut into wedges, a pinch of sugar, salt (optional), and freshly ground black pepper. Drizzle with a little of the reserved vinegar and some olive oil. Top with some coarsely chopped fresh parsley, basil, or mint, if you like, and toss until evenly coated.

rio grande spinach salad

2	red grapefruit
8	ounces spinach, tough stems trimmed and torn into bite-size pieces
1	pint strawberries, hulled
½	cup bottled fat-free red wine vinegar dressing
½	cup sugar
½	teaspoon dry mustard
1½	teaspoons finely grated orange zest
¼	cup fresh red grapefruit juice
1	tablespoon poppy seeds

Finely grate enough zest from 1 grapefruit to equal 1½ teaspoons. Reserve for the vinaigrette.

Section the 2 grapefruit, holding the fruit over a bowl as you cut it to catch the juice. In a salad bowl, combine the grapefruit sections, spinach, and strawberries; toss gently to mix.

In a blender, combine the vinegar, sugar, mustard, orange zest, grapefruit juice, poppy seeds, and the reserved grapefruit zest and blend until mixed, or combine in a jar with a tight-fitting lid and shake until well-blended.

Makes 4 servings
Per serving: 227 calories; 3.8 g protein; 53.6 g carbohydrate; 1.4 g fat; 0 mg cholesterol; 9.6 g dietary fiber; 446 mg sodium

Number of 5 A Day servings: 3.5

quick cook

Cleaning Greens

To thoroughly remove all the dirt and sand from leafy greens, such as spinach and arugula, fill the sink with cool (not cold) water. Swish the greens in the water, allowing the dirt to fall to the bottom of the sink. Drain and repeat one or two times, or until the water is clean.

spinach-citrus salad

2½	pounds fresh spinach, tough stems trimmed and torn into bite-size pieces (about 8 cups)
8	ounces trimmed and sliced white mushrooms (about 2½ cups)
¼	cup sliced scallions
2	slices turkey bacon
2	teaspoons cornstarch
½	teaspoon finely grated orange zest
8	ounces orange juice
⅛	teaspoon garlic salt
⅛	teaspoon freshly ground black pepper
3	oranges, peeled, halved, and sliced
½	medium red bell pepper, cut into thin strips

In a large salad bowl, combine the spinach, mushrooms, and scallions; set aside.

In a large skillet, cook the bacon over medium heat until crisp. Drain on paper towels, then crumble. Wipe out the skillet with a paper towel.

Meanwhile, in a small bowl, blend the cornstarch, orange zest and juice, garlic salt, and black pepper until smooth; pour into the skillet. Cook, stirring, over medium heat, for about 2 minutes, or until the mixture thickens and boils. Cook, stirring, for 2 minutes; remove from the heat. Add the spinach mixture to the skillet and toss until evenly coated. Return the skillet to the heat and cook, tossing, for 30 to 60 seconds longer, or until the spinach is slightly wilted. Return the salad to the bowl and top with the bacon, oranges, and bell pepper.

Makes 4 servings
Per serving: 131 calories; 7 g protein; 25 g carbohydrate; 2 g fat; 5 mg cholesterol; 6 g dietary fiber; 258 mg sodium

Number of 5 A Day servings: 4

wilted spinach salad

1½	pounds spinach, tough stems trimmed (about 6 cups)
1	large yellow bell pepper, cut into strips
1	cup cherry tomato halves
1	pound white mushrooms, trimmed and sliced (about 5 cups)
½	cup bottled low-fat Italian dressing
3	scallions, sliced (about ½ cup)

In a large salad bowl, combine the spinach, bell pepper, cherry tomatoes, and 2 cups of the mushrooms.

Coat a large nonstick skillet with cooking spray. Add the remaining mushrooms and cook over medium-high heat, stirring occasionally, for 5 minutes, or until soft. Stir in the dressing and scallions. Spoon over the spinach and toss gently until evenly coated. Serve hot.

Makes 4 servings
Per serving: 96 calories; 5.1 g protein; 13.3 g carbohydrate; 3.4 g fat; 1.8 mg cholesterol; 2.5 g dietary fiber; 278 mg sodium

Number of 5 A Day servings: 5

penne salad with broccoli rabe

30 minutes or less

1	bunch broccoli rabe, trimmed
¼	cup olive oil
⅓	cup sliced kalamata olives
4	large cloves garlic, thinly sliced
½	teaspoon crushed red pepper flakes
16	ounces penne

In a large pot, bring 6 quarts of water to a boil. Meanwhile, cut the broccoli rabe stalks into 2-inch pieces. Blanch in the boiling water for 1 minute. Transfer to a colander. Keep the water boiling for the pasta.

Heat a large skillet over medium heat. Add the oil, olives, garlic, and crushed red pepper. Cook, stirring, for 3 to 5 minutes, or until the garlic is soft but not browned. Add the broccoli rabe and ¼ cup of the reserved water; cook, stirring, for 3 to 5 minutes longer, or until the broccoli rabe is just tender.

Meanwhile, cook the pasta in the boiling water according to the package directions. Drain. Add the pasta to the broccoli rabe mixture in the skillet and toss to mix well.

Makes 5 servings
Per serving: 479 calories; 14.7 g protein; 72.8 g carbohydrate; 13.2 g fat; 0 mg cholesterol; 2.2 g dietary fiber; 189 mg sodium

Number of 5 A Day servings: 1

sweet potato, pineapple, and pecan salad

Sweet Potato Salad

2	pounds sweet potatoes or yams, peeled and cubed
2	tablespoons fresh lemon juice
1	can (20 ounces) pineapple chunks, drained
1	bunch scallions, sliced
2	ribs celery, chopped (about 1 cup)
¼	cup chopped pecans, toasted

Orange-Honey Dressing

⅓	cup light mayonnaise
1	teaspoon finely grated orange zest
2	tablespoons orange juice
1	tablespoon honey
¼	teaspoon ground ginger
⅛	teaspoon ground nutmeg
	Salt (optional)

To make the sweet potato salad: Bring a large saucepan of water to a boil over high heat. Add the sweet potatoes and cook for 8 to 10 minutes, or just until tender. (Do not overcook.) Drain. Place the potatoes in a large bowl and gently toss with the lemon juice until coated. Add the pineapple, scallions, celery, and pecans, tossing to mix.

To make the dressing: In a small bowl, mix together the mayonnaise, orange zest and juice, honey, ginger, nutmeg, and salt, if desired, until well blended. Spoon over the sweet potato mixture and gently toss until coated. Serve, or cover and refrigerate up to several hours.

Makes 10 servings
Per serving: 151 calories; 2.5 g protein; 31.1 g carbohydrate; 2.8 g fat; 0.3 mg cholesterol; 3.3 g dietary fiber; 1 mg sodium

Number of 5 A Day servings: 2

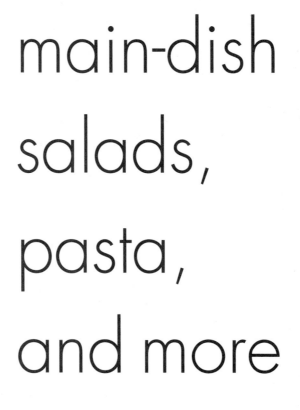

main-dish salads, pasta, and more

asian apple-chicken salad

2	cups cubed cooked chicken breast or firm tofu (not silken)
2	large apples, cored and cubed (about 2 cups)
2	tablespoons fresh lime juice
2	tablespoons apple, orange, or carrot juice
1½	tablespoons light sesame oil
1	tablespoon light soy sauce
1	tablespoon mirin (see below)
1	inch piece of fresh ginger, finely grated
¼	cup chopped fresh parsley
¼	cup chopped fresh cilantro
3	scallions, thinly sliced
1	pound baby spinach

In a large bowl, put the chicken and apples. In a small bowl, mix together the lime juice, apple juice, sesame oil, soy, mirin, and ginger; pour over the chicken mixture. Sprinkle the parsley, cilantro, and scallions over the top and gently toss to mix. (Cover and refrigerate up to several hours, if desired.)

To serve, layer the spinach on a platter and spoon the chicken mixture on top.

Makes 4 servings
Per serving: 244 calories; 25.4 g protein; 18.1 g carbohydrate; 8.3 g fat; 60 mg cholesterol; 5.3 g dietary fiber; 370 mg sodium

Number of 5 A Day servings: 4.5

Cooking Tip

A good alternative for the mirin is a sweet teriyaki-type sauce or dry sherry.

balsamic chicken salad

⅓	cup balsamic vinegar
1	tablespoon Dijon mustard
¼	teaspoon seasoned salt
¼	teaspoon sugar
⅛	teaspoon freshly ground black pepper
12	ounces boneless, skinless chicken breast halves
1	pound sweet onion, cut into 12 wedges
8	cups mixed baby salad greens (about 6 ounces)
2	cups seedless grapes
2	tablespoons thinly sliced fresh basil

Preheat the grill to medium-high.

In a small bowl, whisk together the vinegar, mustard, salt, sugar, and pepper until blended and smooth. Pour 2 tablespoons of the dressing into a cup and brush over the chicken and onion wedges. Let the chicken and onion stand for 5 minutes.

Grill the chicken for 12 to 15 minutes, or until a thermometer inserted in the thickest portion registers 160°F and the juices run clear, turning once. Grill the onion for 3 to 5 minutes on each side, or until soft.

In a large bowl, toss together the salad greens, grapes, basil, and the remaining dressing until evenly coated; transfer to a platter. Cut the chicken into ½-inch-thick slices and arrange over the salad.

Makes 4 servings
Per serving: 227 calories; 21 g protein; 30.6 g carbohydrate; 3.3 g fat; 47 mg cholesterol; 4.7 g dietary fiber; 319 mg sodium
Number of 5 A Day servings: 3.5

california chicken and kiwifruit salad

1½	cups cubed cooked chicken breast meat
¼	cup chopped celery
¼	cup coarsely chopped walnuts
3	tablespoons fat-free mayonnaise
¼	teaspoon salt
4	lettuce leaves
4	kiwifruit, peeled and sliced

In a medium bowl, combine the chicken, celery, walnuts, mayonnaise, and salt, tossing until well-mixed. Line 2 plates with the lettuce and spoon the salad over top. Garnish each serving with kiwifruit.

Makes 2 servings
Per serving: 329 calories; 31.1 g protein; 28.7 g carbohydrate; 10.8 g fat; 79 mg cholesterol; 5.8 g dietary fiber; 244 mg sodium

Number of 5 A Day servings: 1.5

roasted chicken salad with raspberry vinaigrette

½ cup bottled fat-free raspberry vinaigrette dressing

8 cups mixed baby salad greens (about 6 ounces)

1 deli-roasted chicken (about 3 pounds), skin removed and meat cut into large chunks

1 orange or tangerine, sectioned

In a large salad bowl, toss ¼ cup of the dressing with the salad greens until well coated. Top with the chicken and orange segments and drizzle with the remaining dressing.

Makes 4 servings
Per serving: 281 calories; 39 g protein; 12 g carbohydrate; 8 g fat; 100 mg cholesterol; 3 g dietary fiber; 220 mg sodium

Number of 5 A Day servings: 2

warm plum
and smoked chicken salad

2	tablespoons walnuts
2	slices turkey bacon, cut into 1-inch pieces
6	tablespoons balsamic or red wine vinegar
¼	cup olive oil
8	ounces boneless smoked chicken, shredded, or 1½ cups shredded cooked chicken
6	plums, cut into thin wedges
5	scallions, diagonally sliced (about ⅔ cup)
	Romaine, curly endive, or leaf lettuce, torn into bite-size pieces

In a large skillet, cook the walnuts over medium heat, stirring frequently, until lightly toasted. Transfer to a dish. In the same skillet, cook the bacon until crisp. Transfer the bacon to a plate and discard the fat. In the same skillet (do not wipe it out) pour in the vinegar and oil and bring to a boil. Add the chicken, plums, bacon, walnuts, and scallions to the dressing and toss until warm.

To serve, line plates with lettuce and spoon the salad on top.

Makes 4 servings
Per serving: 209 calories; 20.1 g protein; 18.7 g carbo-hydrate; 6.4 g fat; 53 mg cholesterol; 2.5 g dietary fiber; 143 mg sodium

Number of 5 A Day servings: 1

smoked trout salad
with oranges and almonds

2	cups brown rice
4	cups water
8	small oranges
2	tablespoons olive oil
¼	cup chopped chives or scallions
1	small turnip (about 2½ inches across), peeled and cut into thin wedges
1	bunch arugula, trimmed
4	ounces boneless smoked trout, flaked (about 1 cup)
⅓	cup sliced almonds, toasted (see below)

In a medium saucepan, combine the rice and water and bring to a boil over high heat. Reduce the heat to low; cover and simmer for about 40 minutes, or until the rice is tender and water is absorbed.

Meanwhile, peel the oranges and cut into segments. Squeeze the juice from the membrane (white lining) over a small bowl. Whisk the oil into the orange juice; stir in the chives.

Coat a medium nonstick skillet with cooking spray and place over high heat. Add the turnips and cook, stirring, for 3 minutes, or until soft. Remove from the heat. Stir in the orange segments and rice. In a large bowl, toss the arugula with the vinaigrette until evenly coated.

To serve, divide the rice mixture among plates. Top with the arugula and trout; sprinkle with the almonds.

Makes 4 servings
Per serving: 673 calories; 20.6 g protein; 112.1 g carbohydrate; 17.3 g fat; 17 mg cholesterol; 13.7 g dietary fiber; 473 mg sodium

Number of 5 A Day servings: 3.5

Cooking Tip

To toast almonds, spread in an ungreased baking pan. Place in 350°F oven and bake for 7 to 10 minutes or until almonds are light brown, stirring once or twice to ensure even browning.

avocado and smoked turkey salad in bread baskets

Dressing

¼	cup olive oil
3	tablespoons balsamic vinegar
1	tablespoon orange marmalade or preserves
1	clove garlic, finely chopped
½	teaspoon curry powder
¼	teaspoon salt
¼	teaspoon freshly ground black pepper

Bread Baskets

2	loaves French bread (each 12 inches long)
2	tablespoons olive oil
2	tablespoons balsamic vinegar

Salad

8	cups mixed baby salad greens (about 6 ounces)
1	cup cubed smoked deli turkey breast
1	cup peeled, seeded, and cubed papaya
1	cup red or green grapes, halved if large
1	medium red apple, cored and cubed
1	ripe avocado, cut into thin wedges

Preheat the oven to 375°F.

To make the dressing: In a small bowl, whisk together the oil, vinegar, marmalade or preserves, garlic, curry powder, salt, and pepper until blended. Set aside.

To make the bread baskets: Using a serrated knife, cut a 1-inch slice off the top of each loaf of bread. Cut all around the cut side of the bread, ½ inch from the edge. With your fingers, rip out the soft bread to form a ½-inch-thick shell. Repeat with second loaf of bread. In a small bowl, whisk together the oil and vinegar. Brush on the inside of each loaf.

Place the bread directly on the oven rack and bake for 5 minutes. Remove from the oven and cool.

To make the salad: Meanwhile, in a large bowl, combine the salad greens, turkey, papaya, grapes, and apple. Re-whisk the dressing, pour over the salad, and toss until evenly coated. Spoon the salad into the bread baskets and top with the avocado wedges. Cut each bread basket into four portions and serve.

Makes 8 servings
Per serving: 256 calories; 7 g protein; 42 g carbohydrate; 6.7 g fat; 3 mg cholesterol; 5 g dietary fiber; 425 mg sodium

Number of 5 A Day servings: 2

mesclun salad with spicy almonds and turkey

Almonds

1	large egg white
¾	teaspoon ground ginger
½	teaspoon cayenne pepper
¼	teaspoon light salt
1¼	cups slivered almonds

Salad

2	teaspoons sherry vinegar
¼	teaspoon light salt
¼	teaspoon freshly ground black pepper
8	cups mixed baby salad greens (about 6 ounces)
2	ripe medium pears, peeled, cored, and cut into ½-inch cubes
5	ounces deli-roasted turkey breast, cut into ½-inch-thick matchstick strips

To make the almonds: Preheat the oven to 350°F. Coat a baking sheet with cooking spray. In a medium bowl, beat the egg white until soft peaks form. Gently fold in the ginger, cayenne, and salt. Stir in the almonds until coated, then spread evenly on the prepared baking sheet.

Bake for 15 to 20 minutes, tossing every 5 minutes, until the nuts are toasted and crisp. When cool enough to handle, break the almonds into small pieces.

To make the salad: Meanwhile, in a large bowl, whisk together the vinegar, salt, and pepper. Add the salad greens, pears, and turkey; toss until evenly coated with the dressing. Divide the salad among plates. Top each salad with 1 tablespoon of the almonds.

Makes 4 servings
Per serving: 198 calories; 21 g protein; 118.1 g carbohydrate; 5.4 g fat; 47 mg cholesterol; 4.8 g fiber; 195 mg sodium
Number of 5 A Day servings: 2.5

Cooking Tip

The leftover Spicy Almonds can be stored in an airtight container up to 2 weeks.

strawberry chef's salad

⅔	cup fat-free sour cream
¼	cup red wine vinegar
2	scallions, sliced
2 to 3	tablespoons honey mustard
	Salt and freshly ground black pepper
	Boston lettuce leaves
2	pints strawberries, hulled
2	cups assorted fruit, such as grapefruit and orange segments, pineapple chunks, and kiwi slices
8	slices lean deli turkey breast or boiled ham (1 ounce each)
½	cup alfalfa sprouts (about 1½ ounces)

In a small bowl, whisk together the sour cream, vinegar, scallions, and mustard; season to taste with salt and pepper.

Line plates with lettuce leaves. Arrange the fruit, turkey, and sprouts on top. Serve the dressing on the side.

Makes 4 servings
Per serving: 190 calories; 22 g protein; 23 g carbohydrate; 3 g fat; 40 mg cholesterol; 5 g dietary fiber; 170 mg sodium

Number of 5 A Day servings: 3

strawberry and turkey spa salad

30 minutes or less

⅓	cup mango chutney, chopped
2	ounces fat-free plain yogurt
¼	cup fat-free mayonnaise dressing
2	tablespoons fresh lime juice
	Salt and freshly ground black pepper
	Boston lettuce leaves
8	ounces sliced deli-roasted turkey breast
2	pints strawberries, hulled and halved
1	cup seedless red grapes
2	medium ribs celery, sliced (about ¾ cup)
1	small red onion, chopped (about ½ cup)
	Mint sprigs, for garnish

In a small bowl, whisk together the chutney, yogurt, mayonnaise and lime juice; season to taste with salt and pepper. Line a platter or individual plates with lettuce. Arrange the turkey, strawberries, and grapes on top and sprinkle with the celery and onion. Spoon the chutney dressing over and garnish with mint sprigs.

Makes 4 servings
Per serving: 261 calories; 21 g protein; 40 g carbohydrate; 4 g fat; 44 mg cholesterol; 5 g dietary fiber; 282 mg sodium

Number of 5 A Day servings: 3

baked manicotti
with asparagus

make ahead   kid-friendly

8	manicotti noodles
1	package (8 ounces) frozen asparagus spears
8	very thin slices Swiss cheese (¼ ounce each)
8	thin slices low-fat low-sodium boiled ham or smoked turkey breast (½ ounce each)
1	tablespoon olive oil
½	cup frozen chopped onion
2	tablespoons minced shallots
1	tablespoon all-purpose flour
1	cup reduced-sodium chicken broth
2	tablespoons dry sherry
1	package (8 ounces) frozen sliced mushrooms
2	tablespoons finely chopped fresh flat-leaf parsley

Preheat the oven to 350°F. Coat a 7- × 10-inch baking dish with cooking spray.

In a large pot, cook the manicotti according to the package directions; drain. Rinse under cold water, drain, and arrange in single layer on a plate. Place the asparagus in a glass dish; cover and microwave on HIGH for 4 to 5 minutes, or until completely thawed (or cook by steaming). Drain and pat dry with paper towels.

Place a slice of ham on top of each slice of cheese. Place 2 or 3 asparagus spears, tip-to-end, along one side of each ham-cheese stack, then roll up tightly. Insert the rolls into the manicotti. Arrange in the prepared baking dish.

In a large skillet, heat the oil over medium-high heat. Add the onion and shallots and cook, stirring, for about 5 minutes, or until soft. Add the flour and stir until blended. Add the chicken broth and sherry and stir until the sauce comes to a boil. Reduce the heat and simmer until the sauce thickens. Add the mushrooms and parsley and simmer for 5 minutes longer.

Pour the sauce over the manicotti. Cover and bake for 20 minutes. Uncover and bake for 10 minutes longer, or until bubbling and golden.

Makes 4 servings
Per serving: 270 calories; 14.6 g protein; 34.5 g carbohydrate; 8 g fat; 17.1 mg cholesterol; 2.6 g dietary fiber; 426 mg sodium

Number of 5 A Day servings: 1

fettuccine with avocado

16	ounces fettuccine
1	ripe medium avocado, diced
½	cup sun-dried tomatoes, drained and chopped
1	large green bell pepper, diced (about 1 cup)
½	cup chopped fresh basil
3	scallions, chopped (about ½ cup)
¼	cup sherry vinegar
2	tablespoons olive oil

In a large pot, cook the pasta according to the package directions. Drain.

Meanwhile, set aside half the avocado for garnish. In a large bowl, combine all the remaining ingredients and toss until mixed. Add the hot pasta and toss. Spoon the pasta into a serving bowl and garnish with the reserved avocado.

Makes 6 servings
Per serving: 336 calories; 10.5 g protein; 53.4 g carbohydrate; 10.7 g fat; 0 mg cholesterol; 6.9 g dietary fiber; 373 mg sodium

Number of 5 A Day servings: 1.5

pasta salad niçoise with avocado

2	cups pasta shells
¼	cup bottled fat-free Italian dressing
¼	cup chopped fresh basil
2	cloves garlic, minced
¼	teaspoon crushed red pepper flakes
1	can (6 ounces) water-packed tuna, drained and flaked
¾	cup diced tomato
½	ripe avocado, diced
¼	cup thinly sliced red onion
2	tablespoons chopped black olives
4	green leaf lettuce leaves

In a large saucepan, cook the pasta according to the package directions. Drain, then rinse briefly under cold water. Drain.

In a small bowl, combine the Italian dressing, basil, garlic, and crushed red pepper. In a large bowl, combine the pasta, tuna, tomato, avocado, red onion, and olives. Add the dressing and toss until evenly coated. Line plates with the lettuce leaves and spoon the salad on top.

Makes 4 servings
Per serving: 205 calories; 16 g protein; 25 g carbo-hydrate; 5 g fat; 7 mg cholesterol; 3 g dietary fiber; 308 mg sodium

Number of 5 A Day servings: 1

quick cook

Pasta with Cherry Tomatoes and Parsley

Here's a quick and satisfying weeknight supper dish that is sure to please the whole family. Cook up your favorite pasta and keep warm. In a large skillet, cook a few cloves of chopped garlic in a little olive oil over medium heat, until soft. Toss in halved cherry tomatoes (for 4 servings use about 1 pint) and a good amount of chopped parsley. Cook, stirring, until the tomatoes just begin to soften, about 3 minutes. Add the hot pasta and season with salt (optional) and freshly ground black pepper. Cook, tossing, until well mixed. Transfer to a pasta bowl and serve Parmesan cheese alongside. If you like, toss in some shredded cooked chicken, strips of ham, or coarsely chopped cooked shrimp.

bowties with tomato-pepper sauce

16	ounces bowties or penne, preferably tomato-flavored
2	tablespoons olive oil
2	tablespoons minced garlic
1	small onion, chopped
1	large red bell pepper, chopped
2	large tomatoes, seeded and chopped (about 3 cups)
¼	cup fat-free half-and-half
¼	cup freshly grated Parmesan cheese
½	teaspoon freshly ground black pepper

In a large pot, cook the pasta according to the package directions. Drain.

Meanwhile, in a large skillet, heat the oil over medium-low heat. Add the garlic and onion and cook until the onion is soft, adding a little water to the skillet if the mixture seems dry. Add the bell pepper and cook for about 2 minutes, or until tender-crisp. Stir in the tomatoes. Remove from the heat and let cool for 1 or 2 minutes. Return the skillet to the heat. Gradually stir in the half-and-half, Parmesan, and black pepper. Reduce the heat to low and cook until heated through. Serve over the pasta.

Makes 4 servings
Per serving: 570 calories; 19.4 g protein; 98.6 g carbohydrate; 10.7 g fat; 12 mg cholesterol; 3 g dietary fiber; 138 mg sodium

Number of 5 A Day servings: 2

sweet potato–bean burritos

2	large red onions, thinly sliced (about 2 cups)
2	teaspoons sugar
4	medium sweet potatoes, baked, peeled and cut into chunks (about 3 cups)
1	can (15 ounces) black beans, rinsed and drained
½	teaspoon ground cumin
8	flour tortillas (6-inch)
3	tablespoons light margarine, melted

Preheat the oven to 350°F.

Coat a large skillet with cooking spray and place over medium-high heat. Add the onion and sugar; cook, stirring, for 5 minutes, or until the onion is soft. Reduce the heat to medium and cook for 10 to 15 minutes, or until onion is caramelized (deep golden brown). Remove from the heat and stir in the sweet potatoes, black beans, and cumin, mixing gently.

Spoon the potato mixture along the center of each tortilla. Roll up the tortillas, jelly-roll style, and place, seam side down, in an oblong baking dish that has been coated with cooking spray. Drizzle the melted margarine over the burritos.

Cover and bake for 10 to 15 minutes, or until well heated through and crispy on the outside.

Makes 8 servings
Per serving: 194 calories; 6.4 g protein; 31 g carbohydrate; 5.2 g fat; 0 mg cholesterol; 10 g dietary fiber; 353 mg sodium
Number of 5 A Day servings: 1.5

california avocado tacos

Fresh Tomato Salsa

1	medium tomato, diced (about 1 cup)
⅓	cup diced onion
2	teaspoons finely chopped fresh cilantro
½	clove garlic, minced
½	teaspoon minced jalapeño pepper
1 to 2	teaspoons fresh lime juice
	Pinch of ground cumin

Tacos

2	medium green bell peppers, cut into thin strips
2	medium red bell peppers, cut into thin strips
1	medium onion, sliced
1	ripe avocado, cut into 12 wedges
½	cup chopped celery
1	cup lightly packed fresh cilantro leaves
12	flour tortillas (7 to 8 inches), warmed

To make the salsa: In a small bowl, mix together all the ingredients. Set aside.

Coat a large skillet with cooking spray and place over medium heat. Add the bell peppers and onion and cook, stirring, for about 5 minutes, or until the onion is soft.

To assemble the tacos: Fill each warm tortilla with the bell pepper mixture, avocado, celery, and cilantro and top with some tomato salsa. Roll up and serve.

Makes 12 servings
Per serving: 170 calories; 4 g protein; 29 g carbohydrate; 6 g fat; 3 mg cholesterol; 3 g dietary fiber; 167 mg sodium

Number of 5 A Day servings: 1

quick cook

Oven-Roasted Vegetables

Roasting vegetables, such as carrots, turnips, beets, asparagus, and winter squash, intensifies their colors and helps their natural sugars caramelize. The key to success is high heat and uniformly-sized vegetables. You can roast vegetables whole, in chunks, or in small cubes. Depending on the vegetables you choose, the roasting will take between 20 minutes and an hour. Toss with a little olive oil and season with salt (optional) and freshly ground black pepper. Spread the vegetables out in one or more roasting pans and roast at 425°F, tossing occasionally, until richly browned along the edges and tender.

meat
and
poultry

chicken and grapefruit stir-fry

1	grapefruit, peeled
1	can (8 ounces) pineapple chunks in unsweetened pineapple juice
2	tablespoons cornstarch
1	teaspoon light soy sauce
1½	tablespoons vegetable oil
1	clove garlic, minced
8	ounces boneless, skinless chicken breast halves, cut across the grain into slices
4	ounces snow peas, trimmed
2	scallions, sliced diagonally

quick cook

Peeling Garlic

Peeling garlic can be a time-consuming task, but here's an easy short cut. Put the unpeeled cloves of garlic on a work surface. Place the flat side of a large knife on top of the cloves. Press down on the knife to very lightly crush the garlic; lift away the peel. Cut away the small, hard end and discard. Chop or slice, as desired.

Peel the grapefruit and cut into sections, holding the fruit over a small bowl to catch the juice. Drain the pineapple well, reserving the juice. Put the pineapple juice and grapefruit juice into a measuring cup and add enough water to equal 1 cup. Add the cornstarch and soy sauce and stir until smooth.

In a large nonstick skillet or wok, heat the oil over medium heat until hot. Add the garlic and chicken and stir-fry for 5 minutes, or until the chicken is no longer pink and the juices run clear. Add the snow peas and cornstarch mixture; stir-fry until the sauce thickens and boils. Add the grapefruit, pineapple, and scallions; stir-fry until heated through.

Makes 4 servings
Per serving: 165 calories; 14 g protein; 20 g carbohydrate; 3 g fat; 31 mg cholesterol; 3 g dietary fiber; 82 mg sodium

Number of 5 A Day servings: 1.5

chicken oriental

1	tablespoon vegetable oil
1	pound boneless, skinless chicken breast halves, cut into 1-inch chunks
8	ounces asparagus, trimmed and cut into 2-inch-matchstick strips
1	medium red or green bell pepper, cut into thin strips
1	medium onion, sliced
2	tablespoons sugar
¼	teaspoon freshly ground black pepper
2	tablespoons light soy sauce
	Hot cooked rice, for serving

In a large skillet or wok, heat the oil over high heat until hot. Add the chicken and stir-fry for about 4 minutes, or until no longer pink and the juices run clear. Transfer to a plate. Add the asparagus, bell pepper, onion, sugar, and black pepper to the skillet. Stir-fry for about 3 minutes, or until the vegetables are crisp-tender. Return the chicken to the skillet. Sprinkle with the soy sauce; cover and cook, for about 1 minute, or until mixture begins to steam. Serve over rice.

Makes 6 servings
Per serving: 156 calories; 20.1 g protein; 11.6 g carbohydrate; 3.4 g fat; 44 mg cholesterol; 2.5 g dietary fiber; 254 mg sodium

Number of 5 A Day servings: 1

fig, apple, and chicken stir-fry

Sauce

⅔	cup low-sodium chicken broth
2	tablespoons light soy sauce
1	tablespoon water
2	teaspoons cornstarch
½	teaspoon sugar

Stir-Fry

1	tablespoon plus 2 teaspoons canola oil
3	boneless, skinless chicken breast halves (about 4 ounces each), cut into bite-size chunks
8	dried figs, chopped
1	medium red apple, cored and cut into ½-inch cubes
4	ounces snow peas, trimmed
1	medium carrot, cut diagonally into thin slices
2	baby bok choy, cut into 1-inch pieces
1	scallion, sliced
	Hot cooked rice or noodles, for serving (optional)

To make the sauce: In a small bowl, whisk together the broth, soy sauce, water, cornstarch, and sugar until blended and smooth.

To make the stir-fry: Heat a large skillet or wok over high heat until hot. Add 1 tablespoon of the oil and the chicken; stir-fry until the chicken is no longer pink and the juices run clear. Transfer the chicken to a bowl. Add 1 teaspoon oil to the skillet. Add the dried figs, apple, snow peas, and carrot; stir-fry for 3 minutes. Add to the chicken in the bowl. Add the remaining 1 teaspoon oil, bok choy, and scallion to the skillet; stir-fry for 1 minute. Return the chicken mixture to the skillet along with ½ cup of the sauce. Stir-fry until the sauce thickens and boils. Serve with rice or noodles, if desired.

Makes 4 servings
Per serving without rice or noodles: 359 calories; 23.6 g protein; 49.2 g carbohydrate; 9.2 g fat; 49.5 mg cholesterol; 6.6 g dietary fiber; 373.7 mg sodium

Number of 5 A Day servings: 2.5

Cooking Tip

For a spicy stir-fry sauce, add ⅛ teaspoon cayenne pepper to the sauce mixture.

fruited chicken paprika

2	boneless, skinless chicken breast halves (about 4 ounces each), cut across the grain into slices
¼	cup dry white wine
1	scallion, chopped
⅛	teaspoon dried tarragon
	Freshly ground black pepper
⅓	cup fat-free sour cream
¼	teaspoon paprika
¼	teaspoon salt (optional)
2	nectarines, sliced

Place the chicken in a microwave-safe casserole dish. Pour the wine over and sprinkle with the scallion and tarragon; season to taste with pepper. Cover with a lid or plastic wrap (if using plastic wrap, vent at one side). Microwave on high for 2 minutes, or until chicken is no longer pink and the juices run clear. Stir in the sour cream, paprika, salt, and nectarines. Microwave on high for 1 to 2 minutes longer, or until heated through.

Makes 2 servings
Per serving: 262 calories; 30.2 g protein; 25 g carbohydrate; 2.1 g fat; 69 mg cholesterol; 2.5 g dietary fiber; 110 mg sodium

Number of 5 A Day servings: 1

honey-dijon chicken
with peach-cilantro salsa

4	boneless, skinless chicken breast halves (about 4 ounces each)
½	cup bottled fat-free honey-Dijon dressing
	Salt and freshly ground black pepper
4	peaches or nectarines, cubed
¼	cup chopped fresh cilantro
1	small red onion, chopped
	Fresh lime juice

Preheat the broiler.

Place the chicken breasts between two pieces of plastic wrap and pound until ¼-inch thick. Brush on both sides with the honey-Dijon dressing and season to taste with salt and pepper. Place on the rack of the broiling pan. Place 4 to 6 inches from the heat source and broil for about 4 minutes on each side, or until a thermometer inserted in the thickest portion registers 160°F and the juices run clear.

Meanwhile, in a medium bowl, combine the peaches, cilantro, red onion, and lime juice.

To serve, place the chicken on plates and spoon the salsa on top.

Makes 4 servings
Per serving without honey-Dijon dressing: 208 calories; 27 g protein; 17 g carbohydrate; 3 g fat; 66 mg cholesterol; 2 g dietary fiber; 148 mg sodium

Number of 5 A Day servings: 1

orange chicken with citrus salsa

make ahead **kid-friendly**

8	ounces frozen orange juice concentrate, thawed
1	small onion, quartered
½ to ¾	teaspoon crushed red pepper flakes
½	teaspoon ground allspice
½	teaspoon curry powder
¼	teaspoon salt (optional)
⅛	teaspoon freshly ground black pepper
6	boneless, skinless chicken breast halves (about 4 ounces each)
2	grapefruit
2	oranges
½	cup mango chutney, chopped
2	tablespoons diagonally sliced scallion

In a food processor or blender, combine the orange juice concentrate, onion, crushed red pepper, allspice, curry powder, salt, and black pepper. Puree until almost smooth.

Put the chicken into a plastic bag and set in a shallow baking dish. Add two-thirds of the marinade to the chicken and seal the bag, turning to coat. Refrigerate for at least 2 or up to 24 hours. Transfer the remaining marinade to a dish; cover and refrigerate.

Meanwhile, peel the grapefruit and oranges. Cut into sections while holding the fruit over a bowl to catch the juice; coarsely chop the fruit. Add the citrus fruit, chutney, and scallion to the juice in the bowl. Cover and refrigerate about 2 hours.

Preheat the broiler. Remove the chicken from the marinade; discard the marinade. Place chicken on the rack of a broiler pan. Broil 4 inches from the heat source, for 5 minutes. Turn and brush with the reserved marinade. Broil for 7 to 10 minutes longer, or until a thermometer inserted in the thickest portion registers 160°F and the juices run clear. Serve with the citrus salsa.

Makes 6 servings
Per serving: 299 calories; 24 g protein; 43 g carbohydrate; 3 g fat; 59 mg cholesterol; 3 g dietary fiber; 151 mg sodium

Number of 5 A Day servings: 1.5

sesame chicken kebabs

Marinade

⅓	cup dry sherry
⅓	cup light soy sauce
¼	cup dark sesame oil
¼	cup water
1	tablespoon finely grated fresh ginger
1	small clove garlic, minced

Kebabs

20	pitted dried plums
1	can (8 ounces) whole baby corn, drained and cut into 2-inch pieces
1	pound boneless, skinless chicken breast halves, cut into 1-inch pieces
1	large red bell pepper, cut into 1-inch pieces
1	medium red onion, cut into 1-inch pieces
2	tablespoons sugar

To make the marinade: In a small bowl, combine the sherry, soy sauce, oil, water, ginger, and garlic. Divide evenly between two large zip-top plastic bags.

To make the kebabs: Place the dried plums and corn in one bag. Place the chicken in the other bag. Seal the bags and turn to coat evenly. Refrigerate for 3 to 6 hours, turning occasionally.

Preheat the grill to medium-high or preheat the broiler. Drain the chicken, discarding the marinade. Drain the dried plums, reserving the marinade. Thread the chicken, dried plums, corn, bell pepper, and onion alternately onto 4 long skewers. Grill or broil 6 inches from the heat source, turning occasionally, for 10 to 12 minutes, or until the chicken is no longer pink and the juices run clear.

Meanwhile, in a small saucepan, combine the reserved marinade and sugar. Bring to a boil over medium-high heat and cook for 2 minutes, or until the sauce is reduced to a glaze. Just before serving, brush the hot glaze over the kebabs.

Makes 4 servings
Per serving: 459 calories; 30.1 g protein; 49.6 g carbohydrate; 15.7 g fat; 66 mg cholesterol; 5.5 g dietary fiber; 455 mg sodium

Number of 5 A Day servings: 2.5

grilled turkey-mushroom burgers with chutney sauce

1	pound ground turkey breast meat (99% lean)
8	ounces white mushrooms, trimmed and finely chopped
1	medium onion, chopped (about ½ cup)
1	tablespoon Worcestershire sauce
3	tablespoons fat-free plain yogurt
3	tablespoons Major Grey chutney, chopped
4	hamburger buns, toasted and kept warm

Preheat the grill or broiler to medium-high.

In a large bowl, combine the turkey, mushrooms, onion, and Worcestershire until well-blended but not overmixed. Shape into 4 patties about ¾ inch thick. Grill or broil about 4 inches from the heat source, for about 5 minutes on each side, or until a thermometer inserted in the center registers 165°F and the meat is no longer pink. In a dish, combine the yogurt and chutney; serve with the burgers.

Makes 4 servings
Per serving: 319 calories; 23.2 g protein; 32 g carbohydrate; 10.5 g fat; 79 mg cholesterol; 1.9 g dietary fiber; 411 mg sodium
Number of 5 A Day servings: 1

quick cook

Pita Delight Sandwiches

These versatile sandwiches are perfect for brown bag lunches. Coarsely grate or chop a mix of your favorite vegetables, such as carrots, zucchini, scallions, tomatoes, cucumbers, celery, parsley, or radishes, and toss together. Cut a 1-inch slice off one edge of each pita to create a pocket. Tuck a lettuce leaf and a slice of low-fat or fat-free cheese inside each pita and brush with Dijon mustard. Generously stuff the pitas with the chopped vegetables and wrap in aluminum foil, plastic wrap, or waxed paper. For a delicious variation, add some tabbouleh to the vegetable mix.

east meets west stir-fry

¼ cup cold water

2 tablespoons light soy sauce

2 teaspoons cornstarch

1 tablespoon finely chopped fresh ginger

1 large clove garlic, finely chopped

4 ounces boneless pork loin, cut into thin strips

2 medium onions, sliced (about 1½ cups)

1 medium carrot, very thinly sliced

2 medium red or green bell peppers or a combination, cut into 1-inch strips

2 medium ribs celery, sliced (about 1 cup)

6 ounces pitted dried plums (about 1 cup), halved

4 cups hot cooked rice

In small bowl blend the water, soy sauce, and cornstarch until smooth.

Coat large nonstick skillet or wok with cooking spray and place over high heat until hot. Add the ginger and garlic; stir-fry for 1 minute. Add the pork and stir-fry for 2 minutes. Add onions and carrot and stir-fry for 2 minutes. Add the bell peppers and celery; stir-fry for 2 to 4 minutes, or just until the vegetables are crisp-tender. Add the dried plums and toss until heated through. Reduce the heat to medium.

Add the cornstarch mixture to the skillet and stir-fry for about 2 minutes, or until the sauce thickens and boils.

To serve, divide the rice among plates and top with the stir-fry.

Makes 4 servings
Per serving: 495 calories, 15 g protein; 101 g carbohydrate; 3 g fat; 17 mg cholesterol; 7 g dietary fiber; 383 mg sodium

Number of 5 A Day servings: 3.5

pork medallions
with honey-glazed fruit

1	tablespoon vegetable oil
1	tablespoon onion powder
1¾	teaspoons dried thyme
1	teaspoon freshly ground black pepper
¾	teaspoon salt
1	pound pork tenderloin, trimmed and cut into ¾-inch-thick slices
2	large green apples, such as Granny Smith
2	teaspoons vegetable oil
1	cup dried figs, halved
½	cup dry white wine or water
3	tablespoons honey
	Chopped fresh parsley, for garnish

In a cup, stir together the oil, onion powder, thyme, pepper, and salt until blended. Rub on both sides of the pork slices. Peel, core, and cut each apple into 16 wedges.

In a large skillet, heat the oil over medium-high heat until hot. Add the pork and cook for about 2 minutes on each side, or until lightly browned and no longer pink. Reduce the heat to medium-low and cook for 3 to 4 minutes longer, or until firm and slightly pink inside. Transfer the pork to a platter and keep warm.

Add the apples, figs, and wine to the pan. Reduce the heat to medium and cook for about 8 minutes, or until the liquid evaporates, stirring frequently with a wooden spoon and scraping up the browned bits from the bottom of the pan. Add the honey and stir for about 2 minutes, or until the apples are tender and glazed. Spoon the apple-fig mixture over and around the pork, sprinkle with parsley, and serve.

Makes 4 servings
Per serving: 427 calories; 26 g protein; 56 g carbohydrate; 11 g fat; 65 mg cholesterol; 6 g dietary fiber; 480 mg sodium

Number of 5 A Day servings: 1.5

pork tenderloin
with orange-basil sauce

1	teaspoon vegetable oil
1	pound pork tenderloin or turkey breast, trimmed and cut into ¼-inch-thick slices
12	ounces pineapple-orange juice or pineapple juice
2	teaspoons cornstarch
2	cloves garlic, finely chopped, or ½ teaspoon garlic powder
1	teaspoon finely grated orange zest
1½	teaspoons dried basil, crushed
2	oranges, sliced
1	scallion, sliced

In a large nonstick skillet, heat the oil over medium-high heat until hot. Add the pork slices and cook, turning, for 3 to 5 minutes, or until the pork is no longer pink. Transfer the pork to a plate and keep warm. Wipe the skillet dry with paper towels.

In the same skillet, whisk together the pineapple-orange juice, cornstarch, garlic, orange zest, and basil until blended. Bring to a boil over medium-high heat; cook for 2 minutes, or until the sauce thickens slightly and boils. Return the pork and any accumulated juices to the skillet; cook for 1 minute or until heated through.

Arrange the pork and orange slices on plates and sprinkle with the scallion.

Makes 4 servings
Per serving: 232 calories; 25.2 g protein; 20.2 g carbohydrate; 5.2 g fat; 73.7 mg cholesterol; 2 g dietary fiber; 64 mg sodium

Number of 5 A Day servings: 1

mexican steak and fruit skewers

kid-friendly

4	teaspoons chili powder
1	tablespoon ground cumin
¾	teaspoon dried oregano
½	teaspoon freshly ground black pepper
1	pound boneless beef top sirloin, trimmed and cut into 1-inch chunks
1	package (6 ounces) Turkish apricots, nectarines, peaches, or apples
8	ounces pineapple-orange juice
2	tablespoons fresh lime or lemon juice
1	medium red bell pepper, cut into 1-inch pieces
1	small red onion, cut into 1-inch pieces
	Warm tortillas or rice and beans, for serving (optional)

Preheat the grill to medium or preheat the broiler.

In a large bowl, combine the chili powder, cumin, oregano, and pepper. Add the beef and toss until evenly coated. Set aside.

In a small saucepan, combine the dried fruit, pineapple-orange juice, and lime juice. Bring to a boil, then reduce the heat and simmer, stirring occasionally, for 10 minutes, or until the fruit is soft but holds its shape. Drain the fruit, discarding the liquid.

Thread the beef, dried fruit, bell pepper, and onion alternately on skewers. Grill slowly over indirect heat or broil 5 to 6 inches from heat source, turning frequently to prevent the fruit from burning, for 8 to 10 minutes, or until the meat is the desired doneness. Serve with warm tortillas or rice and beans, if desired.

Makes 4 servings
Per serving: 361 calories; 36.9 g protein; 32.6 g carbohydrate; 9.1 g fat; 100 mg cholesterol; 4 g dietary fiber; 119 mg sodium

Number of 5 A Day servings: 1.5

fish

and

shellfish

catfish with tropical fruit salsa

1	can (15¼ ounces) tropical fruit salad, drained and chopped
1	can (8 ounces) low-sodium whole corn kernels, drained
¼	cup chopped red onion or scallions
2	tablespoons diced mild green chiles
2	tablespoons chopped fresh cilantro or parsley
1	pound catfish, red snapper, or cod fillets (about 4 ounces each)
2	tablespoons fresh lime juice
½	teaspoon paprika
	Cilantro sprigs and lime wedges, for garnish (optional)

Coat the broiler pan with cooking spray.
In a serving bowl, mix together the tropical fruit, corn, onion, chiles, and cilantro.

Arrange the fish fillets, skin side down, in the prepared broiler pan. Broil, 4 to 6 inches from the heat source, for 4 minutes; turn. Brush with the lime juice and sprinkle with the paprika. Broil for 3 to 5 minutes longer, or until the fish flakes easily. Transfer the fish to a platter and garnish with cilantro sprigs and lime wedges, if desired. Serve with the tropical fruit salsa.

Makes 4 servings
Per serving: 234 calories; 19.2 g protein; 16.7 g carbohydrate; 9.2 g fat; 53 mg cholesterol; 2.5 g dietary fiber; 246 mg sodium

Number of 5 A Day servings: 1

cioppino

¼	cup olive oil
2	large onions, thinly sliced
1	large green bell pepper, chopped
2	cloves garlic, minced
5	large tomatoes, seeded and chopped (about 3½ cups)
1	cup dry white wine
2	tablespoons tomato paste
1	bay leaf
1	teaspoon fresh thyme or ½ teaspoon dried
	Salt
1	can (6½ ounces) chopped clams
1½	pounds thick fish fillets, such as cod or haddock, cut into 2-inch chunks
8	ounces bay or sea scallops
1	tablespoon chopped fresh basil or 1 teaspoon dried
	Freshly ground black pepper

In a large pot or Dutch oven, heat the oil over medium heat. Add the onions and bell pepper and cook, stirring occasionally, for about 7 minutes, or until the onions are soft. Stir in the garlic and cook for 1 minute. Stir in the tomatoes, wine, tomato paste, bay leaf, thyme, and ¼ teaspoon salt. Bring to a simmer and cook, partially covered, for 10 minutes.

Stir the clams with their juice into the stew. Add the chunks of fish. Cover and simmer for 5 minutes. Stir in the scallops and basil; cover and simmer for 4 to 8 minutes longer, or until the scallops are opaque throughout. Season to taste with salt and black pepper and serve in large shallow bowls.

Makes 6 servings
Per serving: 294 calories; 29 g protein; 14.9 g carbohydrate; 10.7 g fat; 62 mg cholesterol; 3.2 g dietary fiber; 211 mg sodium

Number of 5 A Day servings: 2

scandinavian baked halibut dinner

30 minutes or less

1½	pounds halibut fillets or steaks (about 1½ inches thick)
1	tablespoon all-purpose flour
	Freshly ground white or black pepper
	Juice of 1 large lemon (about 3 tablespoons)
2	tablespoons dry white wine
12	cherry tomatoes
12	small white new potatoes (about 1 pound), steamed (see below)
3	tablespoons chopped fresh dill or 2 teaspoons dried dillweed
	Finely grated zest of ½ lemon
1	tablespoon margarine, melted
	Lemon wedges, for serving (optional)

Cooking Tip

To steam the potatoes, cook, tightly covered, on a steamer rack set over boiling water for 12 to 15 minutes, or until just tender.

Preheat the oven to 425°F.

Cut the halibut into 4 equal pieces. Lightly coat the fish with the flour, shaking off the excess; season with pepper.

Coat a large nonstick skillet (preferably ovenproof) with cooking spray and place over medium-high heat. Add the fish and cook for about 2 minutes on each side. If the skillet is not ovenproof, transfer the fish to a 2-quart shallow baking dish. Sprinkle the fish with the lemon juice and wine. Place the tomatoes and potatoes around the fish and sprinkle with 2 tablespoons of the fresh dill or 1 teaspoon dried.

Bake, uncovered, for about 10 minutes, or until the fish is opaque throughout. Sprinkle the fish with the remaining dill and the lemon zest. Drizzle the margarine over the potatoes. Serve with lemon wedges, if desired.

Makes 4 servings
Per serving: 312 calories; 38.8 g protein; 19.6 g carbohydrate; 7 g fat; 54 mg cholesterol; 2.7 g dietary fiber; 103 mg sodium

Number of 5 A Day servings: 2

fisherman's salmon with rice and tomatoes

12	ounces cooked fresh salmon or 2 cans (7 ounces each), drained
1	tablespoon olive oil
1	tablespoon white wine vinegar
2	teaspoons Dijon mustard
1	tablespoon finely chopped parsley
1	cup cooked rice, chilled
1	cup cooked whole corn kernels, chilled
4	large tomatoes, halved and seeded

Put the salmon into a large bowl and flake it with a fork.

Whisk together the oil, vinegar, and mustard until well blended. Stir in the parsley. Add the rice, corn, and dressing to the salmon and toss until well-mixed. Place the tomato halves on a platter and fill with the salmon mixture.

Makes 4 servings
Per serving with fresh salmon: 289 calories; 24 g protein; 28 g carbohydrate; 10 g fat; 62 mg cholesterol; 3 g dietary fiber; 108 mg sodium

Number of 5 A Day servings: 1.5

steamed salmon with walnut vinaigrette

4	salmon fillets (about 3 ounces each)
1⅓	pounds small red potatoes, quartered
1	pound asparagus, trimmed
1	cup low-fat honey-Dijon mustard vinaigrette
½	cup finely chopped walnuts

Cooking Tip

The salmon, asparagus, and potatoes can be steamed separately in a large pot.

In a three-tier bamboo steamer, place the salmon in one basket, the potatoes in another, and the asparagus in the third. Set over boiling water. Steam for 15 minutes, or until the fish is opaque throughout and the asparagus and potatoes are tender.

Meanwhile, in a small saucepan, combine the Dijon mustard vinaigrette and nuts; cook, stirring, over medium heat until the sauce is heated through.

Arrange the salmon, potatoes, and asparagus on a platter and serve the sauce alongside.

Makes 4 servings
Per serving: 500 calories; 32 g protein; 55 g carbohydrate; 17 g fat; 49 mg cholesterol; 5 g dietary fiber; 346 mg sodium

Number of 5 A Day servings: 2.5

nectarines
with sea scallops

30 minutes or less

2	scallions, sliced
1	clove garlic, minced
8	ounces sea scallops, quartered, or bay scallops
2	medium nectarines, cut into wedges
4	teaspoons fresh lemon juice
	Freshly ground black pepper
1	tablespoon chopped fresh parsley

Layer the scallions, garlic, scallops, and nectarines in two 8-ounce ramekins or ovenproof bowls. Sprinkle with the lemon juice and season with pepper. Cover with a paper towel. Microwave on medium for 3 to 5 minutes, or until the scallops are opaque throughout. Sprinkle with the parsley and serve.

Makes 2 servings
Per serving: 175 calories; 20.8 g protein; 21.3 g carbohydrate; 1.5 g fat; 37 mg cholesterol; 2.7 g dietary fiber; 186 mg sodium
Number of 5 A Day servings: 1

quick cook

Spicy Broccoli with Garlic and Parmesan

Want to serve broccoli to your family, but can't think of anything new? Try this irresistible side dish. Trim a bunch of broccoli and cut into florets (include a generous amount of stem). Cook in 1 inch of boiling salted (optional) water just until tender, about 5 minutes; drain. Meanwhile, in a large skillet, heat a small amount of olive oil over low heat. Add thinly sliced garlic and cook until golden. Add the broccoli along with a bit of crushed red pepper flakes and season very lightly with salt (optional) and freshly ground black pepper. Cook until the broccoli is heated through. Spoon into a serving dish and sprinkle lightly with grated Parmesan cheese.

springtime scallop and asparagus stir-fry

¾	pound asparagus, trimmed and cut diagonally into 2-inch lengths
¾	cup reduced-sodium chicken broth
1	tablespoon cornstarch
1	teaspoon light soy sauce
12	ounces sea scallops, halved
1	cup trimmed and sliced white mushrooms
1	clove garlic
1	teaspoon dark sesame oil
1	cup cherry tomato halves
3	small scallions, chopped
	Freshly ground black pepper
2	cups hot cooked rice

Bring 1 inch of water to a boil in a large saucepan. Add the asparagus and cook, covered, for 3 to 5 minutes, or until crisp-tender. (Do not overcook.) Drain and rinse under cold water. In a small bowl, blend the chicken broth, cornstarch, and soy sauce until smooth.

Heat a large nonstick skillet or wok over high heat until hot. Add the scallops, mushrooms, garlic, and sesame oil and stir-fry for about 4 minutes, or until scallops are opaque throughout. Stir in the cornstarch mixture and cook, stirring, until the sauce thickens and boils. Add the asparagus, cherry tomatoes, and scallions and season to taste with pepper; stir-fry until heated through. Serve over the rice.

Makes 4 servings
Per serving: 246 calories; 20 g protein; 34.2 g carbohydrate; 2.4 g fat; 29 mg cholesterol; 3.1 g dietary fiber; 206 mg sodium

Number of 5 A Day servings: 1.5

grilled southwestern shrimp

4	large tomatoes
2	tablespoons olive oil
2	tablespoons canned chipotle peppers, chopped
2	tablespoons chopped pickled jalapeño pepper
2	ounces tomato juice
2	tablespoons fresh lime juice
1	tablespoon firmly packed brown sugar
2	tablespoons finely chopped fresh parsley
3	tablespoons minced red onion
14	ounces shrimp, peeled and deveined
	Salt and freshly ground black pepper (optional)

Preheat the grill to high.

Halve, seed, and coarsely chop 2 of the tomatoes; put into a medium bowl. Set aside. Cut the remaining tomatoes into 3 thick crosswise slices. Brush one cut surface of each tomato slice with 1 tablespoon of oil. Grill, oiled side down, for 8 to 10 minutes, or until quite soft.

In the bowl of a food processor, combine the grilled tomatoes with the chipotle peppers, jalapeño peppers, tomato juice, lime juice, and brown sugar. Process until a slightly rough puree, then stir the puree into the chopped fresh tomatoes. Stir in the parsley and onion and season with salt, if desired. Set aside.

In a large bowl, toss the shrimp with the remaining oil. Thread the shrimp onto skewers and lightly season with salt and pepper, if desired. Grill for 3 to 4 minutes on each side, or until opaque throughout. Serve the shrimp while hot with plenty of the sauce on the side.

Makes 6 servings
Per serving: 121 calories; 14.9 g protein; 10.6 g carbohydrate; 2.4 g fat; 100 mg cholesterol; 1.9 g dietary fiber; 119 mg sodium

Number of 5 A Day servings: 1

quick cook

Storing Fresh Herbs

Fresh herbs (such as parsley, basil, thyme, rosemary, chives, savory, mint, and cilantro) are highly perishable, so storing them properly is a good idea. Immerse the root ends or stems (cut them if they look brown) in a container in about 2 inches of cold water. Cover loosely with a plastic bag and refrigerate. After a few days, change the water. If stored properly, herbs can last for 5 days.

pasta with shrimp, tomatoes, and feta

2	teaspoons olive oil
4	scallions, chopped (about ⅔ cup)
1	medium green bell pepper, finely chopped
½	cup finely chopped fresh flat-leaf parsley
1	tablespoon finely chopped fresh oregano or 1 teaspoon dried
¼	teaspoon crushed red pepper flakes
	Salt and freshly ground black pepper (optional)
12	ounces medium shrimp, peeled and deveined
4	firm-ripe medium tomatoes, peeled, seeded, and chopped
½	cup dry white wine
1	tablespoon tomato paste
16	ounces penne
2	ounces feta cheese, crumbled

In a large skillet, heat the oil over medium heat. Add the scallions and cook, stirring, for about 3 minutes, or until wilted. Add the bell pepper, parsley, oregano, and crushed red pepper. Season with salt and pepper, if desired. Cook, stirring, for about 6 minutes, or until the bell pepper is soft.

Reduce the heat to medium-low. Add the shrimp and cook for about 4 minutes, or until opaque throughout. Add the tomatoes and cook until they release their juice. Stir in the white wine and tomato paste and cook for about 15 minutes.

Meanwhile, in a large pot, cook the pasta according to the package directions. Drain. In a serving bowl, toss the pasta with the shrimp mixture. Sprinkle the feta cheese over the top and serve.

Makes 6 servings
Per serving: 415 calories; 24 g protein; 64.6 g carbohydrate; 4.9 g fat; 90 mg cholesterol; 1.8 g dietary fiber; 222 mg sodium

Number of 5 A Day servings: 1

red snapper, mushroom, and black olive packets

10	ounces small white mushrooms, trimmed and halved
2	medium tomatoes, diced (about 1½ cups)
¼	cup pitted black olives, such as kalamata or niçoise, halved
2	large cloves garlic, thinly sliced
1	teaspoon dried thyme, crushed
¼	teaspoon freshly ground black pepper
¼	cup dry white wine
2	tablespoons olive oil
4	red snapper or flounder fillets (about 4 ounces each)
3	cups hot cooked rice

Preheat the grill to medium-high or preheat the oven to 425°F.

In a large bowl, combine the mushrooms, tomatoes, olives, garlic, thyme, pepper, wine, and oil.

Place a 12- × 24-inch heavy-duty aluminum foil rectangle on a work surface. Place the fish fillets in the center of the foil, overlapping them slightly; top with the mushroom mixture. Bring the long edges of the foil together and fold the ends over twice. Double fold the short ends to make an airtight packet.

Grill or bake for 25 minutes, or until the fish flakes easily. To serve, using two spatulas, transfer the packet to a platter and carefully open the ends to allow the steam to escape, then open up the top. Serve the rice alongside.

Makes 4 servings
Per serving: 389 calories; 29 g protein; 42 g carbohydrate; 11.7 g fat; 42 mg cholesterol; 3 g dietary fiber; 236 mg sodium

Number of 5 A Day servings: 2.5

baked almond sole
with warm wild rice salad

¾	cup wild rice
1½	cups water
½	cup sliced almonds
½	cup bran flakes
2	large egg whites, lightly beaten
½	cup all-purpose flour
½	teaspoon light salt, divided
½	teaspoon freshly ground black pepper, divided
4	fillets of sole (about 3 ounces each)
1	tablespoon rice vinegar
1	tablespoon olive oil
1	pound spinach, tough stems trimmed (about 4 cups lightly packed)
2	medium apples, cored and cut into thin wedges
1	medium carrot, coarsely grated Lemon slices, for garnish

Heat the oven to 350°F. Coat a baking sheet with cooking spray.

In a medium saucepan, combine the rice and water and bring to a boil over medium-high heat. Reduce the heat; cover and simmer for about 40 minutes, or until the rice is tender and the water is absorbed.

Meanwhile, in a zip-top plastic bag, put the almonds and bran flakes and crush with a rolling pin or mallet to form coarse crumbs. Transfer to a piece of waxed paper. Put the beaten egg whites into a pie plate. In a shallow bowl, mix together the flour, ¼ teaspoon of the salt, and ¼ teaspoon of the pepper. Evenly coat each sole fillet with the seasoned flour, shaking off the excess. Dip the fish into the beaten egg whites, then coat with the almond mixture. Place the fillets on the prepared baking sheet.

Bake the fish for 10 to 12 minutes, or until the fish flakes easily.

Meanwhile, to make the vinaigrette: In a medium bowl, whisk together the vinegar, oil, and remaining salt and pepper. In a large nonstick skillet, put half the spinach, apples, carrot, rice, and 1 tablespoon of the vinaigrette. Cook over medium heat, tossing, until the spinach is slightly wilted and the salad is warm. Remove to a large bowl and repeat with remaining ingredients. Divide the salad and sole among plates. Garnish with lemon slices.

Makes 4 servings
Per serving: 402 calories; 28 g protein; 41 g carbohydrate; 12 g fat; 41 mg cholesterol; 7 g dietary fiber; 326 mg sodium

Number of 5 A Day servings: 1.5

sole with fresh tomatoes and olives

4	ounces fat-free milk
½	cup Panko (Japanese-style bread crumbs, see Cooking Tip, below) or dried fresh bread crumbs
4	sole fillets (about 4 ounces each) Salt and freshly ground black pepper (optional)
2	tablespoons olive oil
1	cup dry white wine
4	firm-ripe medium tomatoes, peeled, seeded, and chopped
8	pitted green olives, sliced Finely grated zest and juice of 1 orange
2	tablespoons chopped fresh tarragon or 2 teaspoons dried
1	tablespoon chopped fresh parsley
¼	teaspoon crushed red pepper flakes
1	tablespoon finely chopped fresh flat-leaf (Italian) parsley, for garnish

Preheat oven to 200°F.

Put the milk and Panko into separate pie plates. Dip the sole fillets, one at a time, into the milk, then coat with the bread crumbs. Sprinkle with salt and pepper, if desired, and set aside.

In a large skillet, heat the oil over medium-high heat. Cook the fillets, in batches if needed, for about 5 minutes on each side, or until the fish flakes easily. Transfer the fish to an ovenproof platter and place in the oven to keep warm.

Add the wine to the skillet and cook, scraping up any browned bits from the bottom of the pan. Add the tomatoes, olives, orange zest and juice, tarragon, fresh parsley, and crushed red pepper; cook over medium-high heat, stirring, for about 15 minutes, or until the sauce thickens.

To serve, spoon the sauce over the fish and sprinkle with the flat-leaf parsley.

Makes 4 servings
Per serving: 310 calories; 25.2 g protein; 20.6 g carbohydrate; 9.9 g fat; 55 mg cholesterol; 2.5 g dietary fiber; 350 mg sodium

Number of 5 A Day servings: 1

Cooking Tip

Panko is available in specialty food stores and in Asian markets.

side
dishes

artichokes stuffed with oriental noodle salad

Salad

4	medium artichokes, top ½-inch cut off
6	ounces Chinese noodles or spaghetti, broken into 2-inch lengths
4	ounces snow peas, cut diagonally into thin strips
1	cup peeled and chopped cucumber
1	medium carrot, coarsely grated
6	radishes, coarsely grated (about ½ cup)
¼	cup thinly sliced scallions

Dressing

¼	cup unseasoned rice vinegar
1½	tablespoons light soy sauce
4	teaspoons peanut oil
1	teaspoon dark sesame oil
2	tablespoons minced fresh ginger
1	tablespoon finely grated orange zest
1	clove garlic, minced
1	teaspoon sugar
⅛	teaspoon cayenne pepper

To make the salad: Bring a large saucepot of water to a boil over high heat. Add the artichokes and cook for about 20 minutes, or until a knife goes in easily. Drain and cool.

Meanwhile, cook the noodles according to the package directions. About 1 minute before the noodles are done, add the snow peas to the water. Drain the noodles and snow peas together in a colander. Briefly rinse under cold water and drain well.

Cut the artichokes lengthwise in half. With the tip of a teaspoon, remove the center leaves and fuzzy choke. Set the artichokes aside.

To make the dressing: In a medium bowl; whisk together the vinegar, soy sauce, peanut oil, sesame oil, ginger, orange zest, garlic, sugar, and pepper.

In a large bowl combine the noodles, snow peas, cucumber, carrot, radishes, and scallions. Drizzle half of the dressing over the noodle mixture and toss until evenly coated.

Place two artichoke halves on each plate. Spoon the noodle mixture into the artichokes, dividing it evenly. Pour the remaining dressing into a small bowl and pass separately to serve as a dip for the artichoke leaves.

Makes 4 servings
Per serving: 335 calories; 12 g protein; 60 g carbohydrate; 7 g fat; 0 mg cholesterol; 7 g dietary fiber; 352 mg sodium

Number of 5 A Day servings: 2.5

baked asparagus
with parmesan cheese

1   pound asparagus, trimmed

1   teaspoon olive oil

1   tablespoon freshly grated
     Parmesan cheese

1½   tablespoons fresh bread crumbs

Preheat the oven to 450°F.

In a medium baking dish, toss the asparagus with the oil and arrange in an even layer. Sprinkle with the Parmesan and bread crumbs. Bake for about 15 minutes, or until the asparagus is tender.

Makes 4 servings
Per serving: 58 calories; 3.4 g protein; 6.8 g carbohydrate; 1.7 g fat; 1 mg cholesterol; 2.5 g dietary fiber; 51 mg sodium

Number of 5 A Day servings: 1.5

quick cook

Gremolata

This zesty Italian condiment, classically used to sprinkle over osso buco (braised veal shanks), is a great way to perk up steamed or grilled vegetables, such as asparagus, broccoli, green beans, bell peppers, or mushrooms. Combine a few tablespoons of chopped fresh parsley with a little minced garlic and some finely grated lemon or orange zest. Sprinkle over the vegetables just before serving.

broccoli and green beans with green sauce

30 minutes or less   make ahead   kid-friendly

8	ounces spinach, tough stems trimmed (about 2 cups tightly packed)
½	cup low-sodium vegetable broth
2	teaspoons rice or white vinegar
½	teaspoon dark sesame oil
¼	teaspoon light soy sauce
½	teaspoon finely grated fresh ginger (optional)
12	ounces green beans, trimmed and sliced (about 2 cups)
1	medium bunch broccoli, cut into small florets (about 2 cups)

In a blender, combine the spinach, broth, vinegar, oil, soy sauce, and ginger (if using), and puree until smooth.

In a large saucepan, bring 1 inch of water to a boil. Add the green beans and broccoli; cook, covered, for 7 minutes, or just until the vegetables are tender. Drain.

To serve, drizzle some green sauce onto each plate and top with one-fourth of the green beans and one-fourth of the broccoli.

Makes 4 servings
Per serving: 54 calories; 3 g protein; 8 g carbohydrate; 2 g fat; 0 mg cholesterol; 2 g dietary fiber; 133 mg sodium

Number of 5 A Day servings: 2.5

green beans with tomato, basil, and goat cheese

1	tablespoon olive oil
2	cloves garlic, minced
1	pound firm-ripe tomatoes, peeled, seeded, and cut into chunks
2	pounds green beans, trimmed
	Salt and freshly ground black pepper (optional)
1	cup lightly packed fresh basil leaves, cut into thin strips
4	ounces mild goat cheese, crumbled

In a large skillet, heat the oil over medium heat. Add the garlic and cook for about 2 minutes, or until golden. Add the tomatoes and cook, stirring, for 5 to 6 minutes, or until the tomatoes are soft. Add the green beans and season with salt and pepper, if desired. Cook, covered, stirring occasionally, for about 7 minutes, or until the green beans are just tender. If the mixture is too watery, uncover, and cook over high heat for about 5 minutes, or until thickened. Add the basil and toss to mix.

Spoon the vegetable mixture into a serving bowl and sprinkle the goat cheese on top.

Makes 8 servings
Per serving: 71 calories; 3.3 g protein; 12.2 g carbohydrate; 2.2 g fat; 0 mg cholesterol; 3.0 g dietary fiber; 13 mg sodium

Number of 5 A Day servings: 2

quick cook

Peeling Fresh Tomatoes

Some recipes, such as uncooked tomato sauce or those with a chopped tomato topping, call for peeled tomatoes. Here's a quick short cut. Cut a shallow X in the bottom of each tomato. Lower carefully into a pot of boiling water; cook for 1 minute, no longer. With a slotted spoon, transfer the tomatoes to a large bowl of ice water. After a few minutes, slip off the skins with your fingers. Seed, chop, or slice as needed.

lemon carrots

 30 minutes or less

make ahead

 kid-friendly

1	package (16 ounces) baby carrots
¼	cup water
1½	teaspoons olive oil
2	tablespoons thinly sliced scallion, plus additional for garnish (optional)
1½	teaspoons fresh lemon juice
1	clove garlic, minced
¼	teaspoon salt
⅛	teaspoon crushed red pepper flakes

In a large nonstick skillet, combine the carrots and water and bring to a boil over high heat. Reduce the heat; cover and simmer for 8 to 10 minutes, or until the carrots are almost tender. Uncover and cook over medium-high heat until the water evaporates. Add the oil and cook, stirring frequently, for about 5 minutes, or until the carrots are lightly browned and just tender. Stir in the remaining ingredients. Cook, tossing, for about 2 minutes, or until carrots are evenly coated. Sprinkle with additional scallion, if desired.

Makes 4 servings
Per serving: 67 calories; 1 g protein; 12 g carbohydrate; 2 g fat; 0 mg cholesterol; 2.6 g dietary fiber; 174 mg sodium

Number of 5 A Day servings: 2

quick cook

Quick Mediterranean Carrot Salad

In less than 15 minutes, you can have this tasty side dish on the table. Coarsely grate some carrots and put into a serving bowl. Drizzle with a little olive oil, squeeze fresh lemon juice over, and sprinkle with a generous amount of ground cumin. Season with salt (optional) and freshly ground black pepper. For a little color, top with chopped parsley or cilantro.

roasted carrots

make ahead **kid-friendly**

1	package (16 ounces) baby carrots
1	small onion, cut into thin wedges
1½	teaspoons olive or vegetable oil
1	tablespoon chopped fresh parsley
¼	teaspoon salt
⅛	teaspoon freshly ground black pepper

Preheat the oven to 450°F. Coat a 9- × 13-inch baking dish with cooking spray.

In the baking dish, toss together the carrots, onion, and oil. Spread to make a single layer. Roast, stirring occasionally, for 20 to 25 minutes, or until the carrots are lightly browned and just tender. Add the parsley, salt, and pepper and toss to coat.

Makes 4 servings
Per serving: 71 calories; 1 g protein; 13 g carbohydrate; 2 g fat; 0 mg cholesterol; 3 g dietary fiber; 174 mg sodium

Number of 5 A Day servings: 2

grilled cherry-vegetable kebabs

make ahead   kid-friendly

½	cup dry white wine
2	ounces orange juice
2	tablespoons finely grated fresh ginger
2	tablespoons brown sugar
½	teaspoon dried thyme, crushed
½	teaspoon salt
	Dash of freshly ground black pepper
1¼	pounds sweet cherries, pitted and halved (about 2 cups)
1	medium green bell pepper, cut into 1-inch pieces
1	small jicama, peeled and cut into 1- x 1- x ½-inch matchstick strips
1	medium onion, cut into 1-inch pieces

In a small bowl, combine the wine, orange juice, ginger, brown sugar, thyme, salt, and pepper until mixed well.

In a large bowl, combine the cherries, bell pepper, jicama, onion, and marinade, tossing to mix. Cover and refrigerate at least 1 hour or up to overnight, tossing occasionally.

Preheat the grill to medium. Thread the cherries and vegetables alternately onto skewers. Grill the kebabs, turning occasionally, for 10 minutes, or until heated through.

Makes 4 servings
Per serving: 139 calories; 1 g protein; 28.3 g carbohydrate; 1 g fat; 0 mg cholesterol; 2.4 g dietary fiber; 276 mg sodium

Number of 5 A Day servings: 2.5

cherokee corn and beans with acorn squash

make ahead **kid-friendly**

1	acorn squash
1	teaspoon canola oil
1	small onion, chopped
1	can (15 ounces) low-sodium chili beans (kidney, black, and pinto bean mix), rinsed and drained
1	can (15 ounces) low-sodium gold and white whole kernel corn, drained
1	can (15 ounces) low-sodium vegetable broth
	Hot cooked rice, for serving

Preheat the oven to 375°F.

Place the squash directly on the oven rack and bake for 15 minutes, or until softened slightly. When cool enough to handle, peel the squash and cut into 1-inch chunks. Set aside.

In a large saucepan, heat the oil over medium heat. Add the onion and cook for 5 to 7 minutes, or until the onion is golden, adding a splash of water to the pan after about 3 minutes to help the onions cook. Add the chili beans, corn, squash, and vegetable broth. Reduce the heat and simmer, covered, for 20 to 25 minutes, or until the squash is tender. Serve over rice.

Makes 8 servings
Per serving: 118 calories; 4 g protein; 24 g carbohydrate; 1 g fat, 0 mg cholesterol; 4 g dietary fiber; 189 mg sodium

Number of 5 A Day servings: 1.5

quick cook

Preparing Fresh Corn

One of the best ways to enjoy the great taste of corn is to cook with fresh corn kernels. First, shuck the corn by peeling off the green husk and pulling off the thin strands of silk. Scrubbing under cold water with a vegetable brush helps loosen any stubborn silk strands. Stand an ear of corn on the work surface, holding it by its end. With a large sharp knife, carefully slice down the length of the corn to cut off the kernels, cutting as close to the cob as possible.

grilled grapes

6	medium clusters seedless grapes
1	teaspoon olive oil
6	sprigs rosemary
6	sprigs thyme

Preheat the grill to medium.

Wash and thoroughly pat the grapes dry with paper towels. With a pastry brush, brush the grapes with the oil. Tuck a rosemary and thyme sprig into each grape cluster.

Grill, turning frequently, for 15 to 20 minutes, or until the grapes develop grill marks and a few start to split.

Makes 6 servings
Per serving: 124 calories; 1.2 g protein; 29 g carbohydrate; 1.8 g fat; 0 mg cholesterol; 1.7 g dietary fiber; 4 mg sodium

Number of 5 A Day servings: 1

quick cook

Storing Vegetables

To keep vegetables in prime condition, store them in the coolest part of the refrigerator or in the crisper drawer. Loosely wrap leafy greens (lettuce, arugula, watercress, and spinach) in paper towels and store in sealed plastic bags (press out as much air as possible). Other vegetables (broccoli, asparagus, green beans, zucchini, artichokes) should be kept in ventilated plastic bags. Refrigerate mushrooms in their original package, in a brown paper bag, or in an open container so they can "breathe." Winter squash (acorn, butternut, Hubbard), potatoes, onions, and garlic are best kept in a cool, dark place.

caramelized onions

1½	tablespoons olive oil
3	pounds yellow onions, sliced
1	teaspoon dried thyme, crushed
1	teaspoon dried rosemary, crushed
	Salt and freshly ground black pepper

In a large skillet, heat the oil over medium heat. Add the onions, thyme, and rosemary and season to taste with salt and pepper. Cook, stirring, for 15 to 20 minutes, or until the onions are soft and golden. Serve hot or warm. (Can be refrigerated in a covered container up to 5 days. Reheat over low heat.)

Makes 12 servings
Per serving: 61 calories; 1 g protein; 10 g carbohydrate 2 g fat; 0 mg cholesterol; 2 g dietary fiber; 3 mg sodium

Number of 5 A Day servings: 2

serving suggestion

Wilted Spinach Salad: Toss fresh spinach with hot Caramelized Onions, sun-dried tomatoes, and pine nuts. Drizzle with warm vinaigrette dressing and toss well.

Enchilada Stack with an Attitude: Layer a corn tortilla with black or pinto beans, diced bell pepper, dabs of salsa, grated sharp Cheddar cheese, and a layer of Caramelized Onions. Repeat layering, then top with a third tortilla. Sprinkle with cheese and bake until hot and melted.

Smothered Sea Bass: Poach sea bass or other firm white fish and serve on a bed of Caramelized Onions with steamed baby carrots and fresh dill sprigs over all.

Royal Stuffed Bakers: Spoon Caramelized Onions into baked potatoes instead of the usual butter and sour cream. Sprinkle with pepper.

Portobello "Steak" and Onions: Grill or cook thick slices of portobello mushrooms in olive oil and serve (with its juice) over Caramelized Onions.

crispy beer-batter onion rings

1	cup all-purpose flour
1	teaspoon paprika
¾	teaspoon salt
¼	teaspoon freshly ground pepper
1	cup beer (non-alcoholic or regular)
3	large onions, cut into ½-inch-thick round slices, rings separated
1	tablespoon vegetable oil

Cooking Tip

The onion rings can be pan-fried, placed on baking sheets, and set aside up to several hours ahead.

Preheat the oven to 425°F.

In a large bowl, mix together the flour, paprika, salt, and pepper. With a whisk, stir in the beer until the foam subsides.

Add the onion rings to the batter, tossing to coat evenly. With tongs, lift out the onion rings, a few at a time, allowing the excess batter to drip off. Place on a plate.

In a large nonstick skillet, heat the oil over medium-high heat until hot. Place a single layer of onion rings in the skillet and cook for about 1½ minutes on each side, or until browned. Transfer the onion rings as they brown to ungreased baking sheets. Repeat with the remaining onion rings.

Bake the onion rings for 6 minutes, or until crisp.

Makes 6 servings
Per serving: 155 calories; 4 g protein; 29 g carbohydrate; 3 g fat; 0 mg cholesterol; 3 g dietary fiber; 5 mg sodium

Number of 5 A Day servings: 1

roasted vegetables and fruit with citrus-thyme vinaigrette

1	pound small red-skinned potatoes, cut into 1-inch wedges
8	ounces baby carrots
8	ounces shallots, cut into ¾-inch wedges
½	teaspoon olive oil
¼	teaspoon salt
¼	teaspoon freshly ground black pepper
1	medium red bell pepper, cut into 1-inch pieces
1	medium yellow bell pepper, cut into 1-inch pieces
24	lemon- or orange-flavored pitted dried plums
2	tablespoons olive oil
1	clove garlic, minced
2	tablespoons fresh lemon juice
2	tablespoons chopped fresh thyme or ½ teaspoon dried
2	teaspoons Dijon mustard
2	teaspoons honey

Preheat the oven to 450°F. Coat a large baking sheet with cooking spray.

In a large bowl, toss together the potatoes, carrots, shallots, oil, salt, and black pepper until evenly coated. Spread in a single layer on the prepared baking sheet. Roast for 15 minutes; stir in the bell peppers and roast for 10 minutes. Add the dried plums and roast, stirring once, for 5 to 10 minutes longer, or until the dried plums are heated through.

Meanwhile, heat the oil in a small saucepan over medium heat. Add the garlic and cook for 2 minutes, or until fragrant. Remove from the heat. Stir in the lemon juice, thyme, mustard, and honey.

To serve, place the vegetable mixture in a serving bowl, drizzle with the dressing, and toss until coated.

Makes 8 servings
Per serving: 403 calories; 3.9 g protein; 92.3 g carbohydrate; 5.7 g fat; 0 mg cholesterol; 17.3 g dietary fiber; 52 mg sodium

Number of 5 A Day servings: 2

potato–double cheese gratin

make ahead

1	pound all-purpose potatoes, peeled and sliced
1	clove garlic, minced
16	ounces fat-free milk
¼	teaspoon salt
2	tablespoons water
1	teaspoon cornstarch
⅓	cup coarsely grated Swiss cheese
½	cup dried bread crumbs
2	tablespoons freshly grated Parmesan cheese

Preheat the oven to 350°F.

In a large saucepan, combine the potatoes, garlic, milk, and salt. Bring to a simmer over medium heat and cook for about 8 minutes, or until potatoes are almost tender.

Meanwhile, in a cup, blend the water and cornstarch until smooth. Stir into the simmering potato mixture; cook until the liquid thickens slightly. Remove from the heat and stir in the Swiss cheese. Transfer the potato mixture to a small baking dish. Combine bread crumbs and Parmesan; sprinkle over the potato mixture.

Bake the gratin until the top is browned and the mixture is bubbly. Let rest for 20 minutes before serving.

6 servings
Per serving: 167 calories; 8 g protein; 26 g carbohydrate; 3 g fat; 10 mg cholesterol; 2 g dietary fiber; 278 mg sodium

Number of 5 A Day servings: 1

quick cook

Pan-Roasted Potatoes

Who can resist a helping (or two) of crispy potatoes? Pan-roasting is an easy way to turn out any size batch of potatoes with minimal effort. Cut small red or white potatoes in half. In a large roasting pan, toss potatoes with a little oil, salt (optional), freshly ground black pepper and, if you like, some fresh or dried rosemary or thyme. Roast the potatoes at 425°F until crispy on the outside and very tender on the inside, about 30 minutes, tossing occasionally with a spatula. If you prefer, roast them several hours ahead; re-crisp in a hot oven.

Balsamic Chicken Salad, p. 129

main-dish salads

main-dish salads

opposite: Avocado and Smoked Turkey Salad

  in Bread Baskets, p. 134

top: Roasted Chicken Salad with Raspberry

  Vinaigrette, p. 131

bottom: Strawberry Chef's Salad, p. 136

meat and poultry

opposite, top: Chicken and Grapefruit
   Stir-Fry, p. 146

opposite, bottom: Pork Tenderloin with Orange-
   Basil Sauce, p. 156

top: Fig, Apple, and Chicken Stir-Fry, p. 148

bottom: Mexican Steak and Fruit Skewers, p. 157

meat and poultry

fish and shellfish

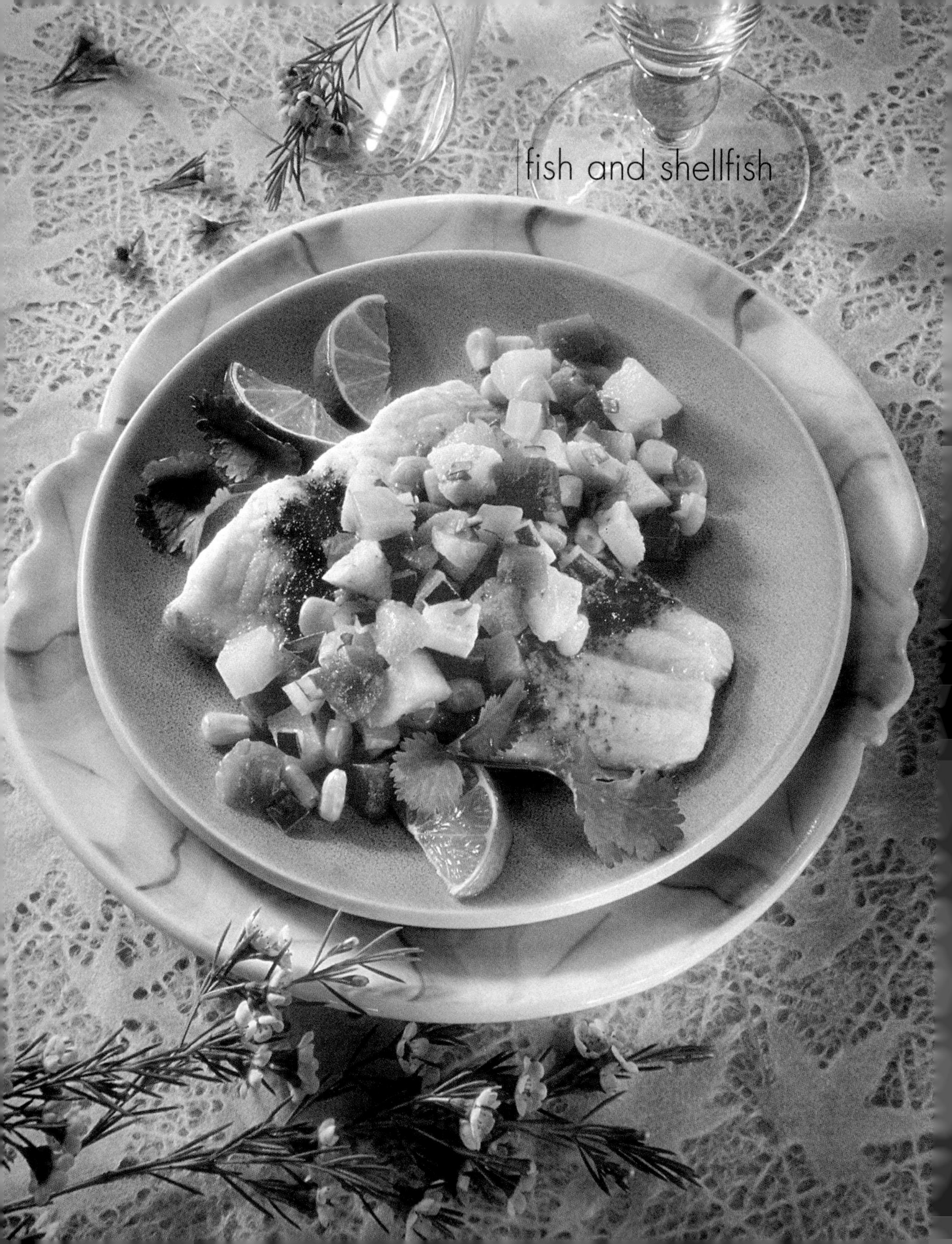

opposite: Catfish with Tropical Fruit Salsa, p. 160

top: Grilled Southwestern Shrimp, p. 167

bottom: Scandinavian Baked Halibut Dinner, p. 162

fish and shellfish

fish and shellfish

194

opposite, top: Baked Almond Sole

with Warm Wild Rice Salad, p. 170

opposite, bottom: Pasta with Shrimp, Tomatoes,

and Feta, p. 168

top: Grilled Cherry-Vegetable Kebabs, p. 180

bottom: Artichokes Stuffed with Oriental

Noodle Salad, p. 174

side dishes

side dishes

top: Caramelized Onions, p. 183

bottom: Roasted Vegetables and Fruit with

Citrus-Thyme Vinaigrette, p. 185

opposite: Grilled Grapes, p. 182

side dishes

side dishes

top: Garden-Style Risotto, p. 210

opposite, top: Orange-Sesame Couscous, p. 208

opposite, bottom: Spaghetti Squash with Chunky

Tomato-Garlic Sauce, p. 205

side dishes

desserts

opposite: Pear-Strawberry Trifle, p. 223

top: Spiced Grapes with Mango,

Papaya, and Pineapple, p. 220

bottom: Watermelon-Blueberry

Banana Split, p. 217

desserts

top: Pear and Cranberry Crisp, p. 224

bottom: No-Guilt Watermelon "Cake", p. 226

skillet sweet potatoes

1	pound sweet potatoes, peeled and cut into ½-inch-thick slices
½	teaspoon finely grated orange zest
4	ounces orange juice
2	tablespoons firmly packed brown sugar or molasses
1	tablespoon margarine, melted
½	teaspoon pumpkin pie spice
¼	teaspoon salt

In a large skillet, combine the sweet potatoes with enough boiling water to cover. Cover and cook, for about 10 minutes, or until the sweet potatoes are tender. Drain well.

Meanwhile, in a small bowl, combine all the remaining ingredients. Return the potatoes to the skillet and pour the sauce over. Cook, stirring, over medium heat for about 6 minutes, or until the sweet potatoes are glazed.

Makes 4 servings
Per serving: 177 calories; 4 g protein; 35 g carbohydrate; 3 g fat; 0 mg cholesterol; 4 g dietary fiber; 174 mg sodium

Number of 5 A Day servings: 2

---

twice-baked yams

3	pounds small sweet potatoes or yams (about 8)
1	can (8 ounces) crushed pineapple in juice, drained
½	cup golden raisins
1	tablespoon packed brown sugar
1	teaspoon vanilla extract
¼	teaspoon ground cinnamon
2	tablespoons chopped pecans
1	cup miniature marshmallows

Preheat the oven to 375°F.

Place the potatoes on a baking sheet and bake for about 1 hour, or until tender. Let cool 15 minutes. Cut a thin slice off the top of each potato. Carefully scoop the pulp into a large bowl, leaving the shells intact. Mash the potatoes. Stir in the pineapple, raisins, brown sugar, vanilla, and cinnamon. Spoon the potato mixture into the shells; sprinkle with the pecans and marshmallows.

Bake for 15 minutes, or until heated through.

Makes 8 servings
Per serving: 255 calories; 3.2 g protein; 59 g carbohydrate; 1.5 g fat; 0 mg cholesterol; 7.7 g dietary fiber; 17 mg sodium

Number of 5 A Day servings: 1

sweet potato–
cranberry galette

2	tablespoons margarine or butter
1	tablespoon olive oil
1	large onion, chopped (about 1 cup)
6	ounces dried cranberries (about 1 cup)
¼	cup firmly packed brown sugar
1	tablespoon ground ginger
2	sweet potatoes or yams (about 1¼ pounds each), peeled and very thinly sliced (see below)

Cooking Tip

A food processor makes quick work out of very thinly slicing potatoes.

Preheat the oven to 400°F. Line a 9-inch round cake pan with aluminum foil and coat with cooking spray.

In a medium skillet, melt the margarine with the oil over medium heat. Add the onion and cook, stirring, for about 5 minutes, or until soft. Stir in the cranberries, brown sugar, and ginger.

Spoon 1 tablespoon of the cranberry mixture into the center of the prepared pan. Arrange one-third of the sweet potato slices in concentric circles, slightly overlapping them. Spread half of the remaining cranberry mixture over the potatoes. Top with half of the remaining sweet potato slices. Spoon the remaining cranberry mixture over and then top with the remaining sweet potatoes. Coat a sheet of foil with cooking spray and tightly cover the pan.

Bake for 40 minutes. Uncover the galette and bake for 20 minutes longer, or until the top is brown and crisp and the potatoes are tender. Place a flat serving plate on top of the cake pan and invert. Serve hot or warm.

Makes 8 servings
Per serving: 236 calories; 2 g protein; 47 g carbohydrate; 5 g fat; 0 mg cholesterol; 7.4 g dietary fiber; 53 mg sodium

Number of 5 A Day servings: 2

spaghetti squash with chunky tomato-garlic sauce

make ahead

kid-friendly

1	large spaghetti squash, cut lengthwise in half
1	tablespoon olive oil
5	firm-ripe medium tomatoes, peeled, seeded, and chopped
1	clove garlic, crushed with the side of a chef's knife
¼	cup balsamic vinegar
	Salt and freshly ground black pepper (optional)
¼	cup freshly grated Parmesan cheese
½	cup lightly packed fresh basil leaves, cut into thin strips

Preheat the oven to 350°F.

Wrap the squash halves in aluminum foil and place in a baking dish. Bake for 45 minutes, or until tender. Reduce the oven temperature to 200°F.

Meanwhile, in a large skillet, heat the oil over medium heat. Add the tomatoes and garlic and cook, stirring, for 20 to 30 minutes, or until the mixture thickens. Add the vinegar and season with salt and pepper, if desired. Carefully open the foil (be careful of any steam) and remove the squash. Scoop out the seeds and stringy fibers; discard. With a large spoon, scoop the flesh into a bowl. Using two forks, pull apart the flesh so it separates into spaghetti-like strands.

Transfer the spaghetti squash to a serving dish. Spoon the tomato sauce over the squash and sprinkle with the Parmesan and basil.

Makes 4 servings
Per serving: 158 calories; 5.6 g protein; 22.3 g carbohydrate; 6.8 g fat; 5 mg cholesterol; 4.6 g dietary fiber; 162 mg sodium

Number of 5 A Day servings: 2

curried rice with roasted carrots and apricots

3	cups basmati rice
4	medium carrots, sliced (about 2 cups)
½	cup low-sodium chicken or vegetable broth
½	cup dried apricots, diced
2	tablespoons walnuts or sliced almonds, toasted (optional)
2	tablespoons curry powder

Preheat the oven to 400°F.

Cook the rice according to the package directions. Keep hot.

Meanwhile, put the carrots into a roasting pan and cover with aluminum foil. Roast for 25 to 35 minutes, or until the carrots are tender. Stir the chicken broth, apricots, walnuts, and curry powder into the rice. Heat over low heat until heated through. Transfer the rice mixture to a serving dish, top with the carrots, and serve.

Makes 4 servings
Per serving: 625 calories; 12 g protein; 134 g carbohydrate; 4 g fat; 0 mg cholesterol; 6 g dietary fiber; 124 mg sodium

Number of 5 A Day servings: 1.5

moroccan couscous with mushrooms

¼ cup olive oil, divided

12 ounces small portobello mushrooms, stems removed and caps sliced

½ teaspoon salt, divided

¼ teaspoon freshly ground black pepper, divided

1 small onion, thinly sliced

1 teaspoon ground cumin

¼ teaspoon ground cinnamon

12 ounces orange juice

1¼ cups water

1½ cups couscous

Sliced scallions, golden raisins, and sliced almonds, for garnish (optional)

In a large skillet, heat 2 tablespoons of the oil over medium-high heat. Add the portobellos; sprinkle with ¼ teaspoon of the salt and ⅛ teaspoon of the pepper. Cook, stirring occasionally, for about 7 minutes, or until tender. Transfer the mushrooms to a plate and keep warm.

Add the remaining oil to the skillet. Add the onion, cumin, and cinnamon; cook, stirring, for about 5 minutes, or until the onion is tender. Add the orange juice and briskly simmer for about 5 minutes, or until the liquid is reduced to 1 cup. Remove from the heat and keep hot.

Meanwhile, prepare the couscous: In a medium saucepan, bring the water to a boil. Stir in the couscous, the remaining ¼ teaspoon salt, and the remaining ⅛ teaspoon pepper. Remove from the heat; cover and let stand for 10 minutes. Fluff the couscous with a fork. Stir in the scallions, golden raisins, and almonds, if desired.

To serve, divide the couscous among plates, top each portion with the portobellos, and drizzle with the sauce.

Makes 4 servings
Per serving: 453 calories; 12 g protein; 70 g carbohydrate; 9 g fat; 0 mg cholesterol; 4 g dietary fiber, 304 mg sodium

Number of 5 A Day servings: 1.5

orange-sesame couscous

8	ounces fresh orange juice (about 3 oranges)
½	cup chopped red or green bell pepper
1	teaspoon dark sesame oil
⅛	teaspoon salt
⅔	cup couscous (precooked semolina)
1	orange, peeled and cut into bite-size pieces
3	tablespoons chopped scallion

In a medium saucepan, combine the orange juice, bell pepper, sesame oil, and salt. Bring just to a boil; stir in the couscous. Cover and remove from the heat. Let stand for 5 minutes, then fluff the couscous with a fork. Stir in the orange pieces and scallion.

Makes 3 servings
Per serving: 231 calories; 6 g protein; 47 g carbohydrate; 2 g fat; 0 mg cholesterol; 3 g dietary fiber; 95 mg sodium

Number of 5 A Day servings: 1

serving suggestion

Serve with grilled or broiled salmon steaks.

polenta, spinach, and mushroom lasagna

1	tablespoon olive oil
1	pound white mushrooms, trimmed and thinly sliced
½	cup freshly grated Parmesan cheese
1	package (10 ounces) frozen chopped spinach, thawed and squeezed dry
¼	cup prepared pesto, plus additional for serving (optional)
1	cup instant polenta or yellow cornmeal
	Tomato sauce, for serving (optional)

Make-Ahead Tip

Cover the lasagna with aluminum foil; refrigerate up to 24 hours. To reheat, bake in a preheated 375°F oven for about 30 minutes, or until heated through.

Preheat the oven to 375°F. Lightly coat a 9-inch pie plate with cooking spray.

In a large nonstick skillet, heat the oil over high heat. Add the mushrooms and cook, stirring, for about 10 minutes, or until tender and lightly browned. Transfer 1 cup of the mushrooms to a small bowl and stir in 1 tablespoon of the Parmesan; set aside.

Stir the spinach and pesto into the mushrooms in the skillet; cook for about 2 minutes, or until heated through. Set aside. Cook the polenta according to the package directions. Remove from the heat and stir in the remaining cheese.

Spread half of the polenta in the prepared pie plate. Spoon the mushroom-spinach mixture over the polenta. With a narrow metal spatula, evenly spread the remaining polenta on top. Cover with the reserved mushroom mixture.

Bake for about 10 minutes, or until heated through. Let stand 5 minutes before cutting into wedges. Serve on a bed of tomato sauce or top with a dollop of pesto, if desired.

Makes 4 servings
Per serving (without tomato sauce): 523 calories; 18 g protein; 77 g carbohydrate; 15.9 g fat; 15 mg cholesterol; 12 g dietary fiber; 287 g sodium

Number of 5 A Day servings: 3.5

garden-style risotto

1	can (14½ ounces) low-sodium chicken broth
1¾	cups water
2	cloves garlic, finely chopped
1	teaspoon dried basil, crushed
½	teaspoon dried thyme, crushed
1	cup Arborio rice
10	ounces spinach, tough stems trimmed and torn into bite-size pieces (about 3 cups tightly packed)
2	medium carrots, coarsely grated (about 1½ cups)
3	tablespoons freshly grated Parmesan cheese
	Chopped yellow tomato and red onion, for garnish (optional)

In large saucepan, combine the chicken broth, water, garlic, basil, and thyme. Bring to a boil over medium-high heat. Coat a large saucepan (preferably nonstick) with cooking spray and place over medium heat. Add the rice and cook, stirring constantly, for 2 minutes, or until the rice is golden. Pour 1 cup of the boiling broth into the rice. Cook, stirring constantly, until the broth is almost absorbed. Add enough of the remaining broth to barely cover the rice. Cook, stirring constantly, until the broth is almost absorbed. Continue adding the broth as directed, adding the spinach and carrots with the last addition of broth. Cook, stirring constantly, for 3 to 5 minutes, or until the broth is almost absorbed and rice and vegetables are tender. (Do not overcook. Risotto should have a creamy texture.) Stir in the Parmesan. Spoon into a serving bowl, garnish with yellow tomatoes and red onion, if desired, and serve.

Makes 6 servings
Per serving: 187 calories; 6.2 g protein; 34.9 g carbohydrate; 1.8 g fat; 4.9 mg cholesterol; 2.2 g dietary fiber; 102 mg sodium

Number of 5 A Day servings: 1

Variation

Garden Pilaf: Substitute 1 cup regular long-grain white rice for the Arborio rice and reduce the water ½ cup. Brown the rice as directed. Carefully stir the browned rice into the boiling broth. Reduce the heat to low; cover and cook for 15 minutes. Stir in the vegetables; cover and cook for 4 to 5 minutes, or until the rice and vegetables are tender. Stir in the Parmesan.

confetti plum-pasta salad

8	ounces colored corkscrew pasta
½	medium red bell pepper, cut into strips
½	medium yellow bell pepper, cut into strips
¾	cup peeled and diced jicama
½	cup chopped red onion
4	plums, sliced
2	tablespoons chopped fresh basil
2	teaspoons diced pimiento
1	teaspoon finely grated fresh ginger
3	tablespoons rice or white wine vinegar
1	tablespoon vegetable oil
	Salt and freshly ground black pepper

Cook the pasta according to the package directions. Drain. Rinse briefly under cold water and drain.

In a large bowl, toss together the pasta, red and yellow bell peppers, jicama, onion, and plums.

In a small bowl, whisk together all the basil, pimiento, ginger, vinegar, oil, salt, and pepper until blended. Drizzle the dressing over the salad and toss until evenly coated.

Makes 6 servings
Per serving: 182 calories; 5.5 g protein; 34.1 g carbohydrate; 2.4 g fat; 0 mg cholesterol; 1.6 g dietary fiber; 2 mg sodium

Number of 5 A Day servings: 1

Cooking Tip

> If you grow a bumper crop of mint in your garden, substitute it for the basil.

desserts

baked apple fritters

kid-friendly

1	package active dry yeast
¼	cup warm water (105°–115°F)
6	ounces low-fat milk, scalded
4	tablespoons margarine
¼	cup granulated sugar
½	teaspoon salt
3¼	cups all-purpose flour
1½	teaspoons ground cinnamon
1	large egg
2	cups peeled and chopped apples (about 2 cups)

Confectioners' Sugar Glaze

1	cup confectioners' sugar
2	tablespoons hot water

Cooking Tip

Substitute 1 can (20 ounces) apple slices, drained and chopped, for the fresh apples. Prepare as directed.

Coat a large baking sheet with cooking spray. In a cup, combine the yeast and warm water, stirring to dissolve. Let stand about 5 minutes, or until foamy.

In a large bowl, stir together the hot milk, margarine, granulated sugar, and salt until the margarine melts. With a mixer on low speed, add 1 cup of the flour to the milk mixture, beating until combined. Increase the speed to medium and beat for 3 minutes, scraping the bowl occasionally. Beat in the yeast mixture, cinnamon, and egg until well-blended.

Attach the dough hook to the mixer. On low speed, gradually add the remaining flour to make a sticky dough. Continue kneading for 5 minutes, or until the dough is smooth and satiny. Mix in the apples. (Or alternately, stir in the remaining flour with a wooden spoon, then turn the dough onto a lightly floured surface and knead.)

Place the dough in a large bowl coated with cooking spray. Coat the top of the dough with cooking spray. Cover and let rise in a warm place for about 1½ hours, or until doubled in volume. Punch the dough down and let rest for 10 minutes. Drop ¼ cupfuls of the dough onto the prepared baking sheet to make 16 fritters. Let rise for about 1 hour, or until doubled in volume.

Meanwhile, preheat the oven to 350°F. Bake the fritters for about 10 minutes, or until golden brown. Cool slightly.

Prepare the glaze: In a small bowl, stir together the confectioners' sugar and water until smooth. Brush over the warm fritters. Serve warm or at room temperature.

Makes 4 servings (16 fritters)
Per serving (4 fritters): 720 calories; 16 g protein; 132 g carbohydrate; 16 g fat; 56 mg cholesterol; 4 g dietary fiber; 468 mg sodium

Number of 5 A Day servings: 1

banana-apple sherbet

make
ahead

kid-
friendly

2	large ripe bananas
1	tablespoon fresh lemon juice
1½	cups applesauce
3	tablespoons honey

Cut the bananas into 1-inch-thick slices; dip in the lemon juice to prevent browning. Arrange the bananas on a baking sheet. Place in the freezer for about 4 hours, or until firm.

Pour the applesauce into an ice cube tray. Place in the freezer for about 4 hours, or until firm.

In a food processor, combine the frozen bananas and applesauce and puree until almost smooth. Add the honey and process until smooth and creamy. Scoop into serving dishes and serve immediately.

Makes 4 servings
Per serving: 151 calories; 0.9 g protein; 39.7 g carbohydrate; 0.4 g fat; 0 mg cholesterol; 12.8 g dietary fiber; 3 mg sodium

Number of 5 A Day servings: 1

quick cook

One-Ingredient Sorbet

Here's a simple way to make delicious, creamy sorbet without an ice-cream maker. Drain one or more large cans of fruit that are packed in light syrup (such as peaches, apricots, and pears), reserving half the syrup. Coarsely chop the fruit and spread out in a shallow metal baking pan; pour in the reserved syrup. Place in the freezer until partially frozen, about 2 hours. Puree the fruit in a food processor, in batches if necessary, until smooth. Return the puree to the baking pan and freeze until firm enough to scoop, about 1 hour longer.

warm blueberry cobbler

Fruit Filling

½	cup sugar
2	tablespoons cornstarch
4	cups fresh or frozen blueberries (about 2 pints)
1	teaspoon fresh lemon juice

Biscuit Topping

1	cup all-purpose flour
1	tablespoon sugar
1½	teaspoons baking powder
4	ounces reduced-fat milk
3	tablespoons vegetable oil

Preheat the oven to 400°F.

To make the fruit filling: In a large saucepan, mix together the sugar and cornstarch. Stir in the blueberries and lemon juice. Cook, stirring constantly, over medium-high heat until the mixture thickens and boils. Boil, stirring, for 1 minute. Pour the fruit mixture into an ungreased small baking dish. Cover to keep hot.

To make the topping: In a medium bowl, whisk together the flour, sugar, and baking powder. Add the milk and oil, stirring with a wooden spoon until a dough forms. Drop the dough onto the hot fruit to make 6 mounds.

Bake for 25 to 30 minutes, or until the biscuit topping is golden brown. Serve warm.

Makes 6 servings
Per serving: 281 calories; 3.5 g protein; 52 g carbohydrate; 7.5 g fat; 1 mg cholesterol; 3 g dietary fiber; 139 mg sodium

Number of 5 A Day servings: 1

quick cook

Berries Year-Round

The summer season brings a bounty of luscious, sweet, and reasonably priced berries, but alas, the season is short. Why not freeze some of nature's bounty for future use? Wash the berries and pat dry with paper towels. Spread out the berries in a jelly-roll pan and place in the freezer until hard. Return them to their original containers, wrap in heavy-duty aluminum foil, and place in zip-top plastic freezer bags. Label and date the bags and freeze the berries up to 6 months. When frozen this way, the berries will not stick together.

watermelon-blueberry banana split

2	large ripe bananas
8	scoops seedless watermelon (see Cooking Tip, below)
1	pint blueberries
½	cup low-fat vanilla yogurt
¼	cup crunchy cereal nuggets

Cut the bananas crosswise in half; cut each piece lengthwise in half. For each serving, place 2 pieces of banana against the sides of a long shallow dessert dish. Place a scoop of watermelon at each end of the dish. Fill the center with blueberries. Stir the yogurt until smooth; spoon over the watermelon. Sprinkle with the cereal nuggets.

Makes 4 servings
Per serving: 186 calories; 4 g protein; 44 g carbohydrate; 1 g fat; 1 mg cholesterol; 3 g dietary fiber; 66 mg sodium

Number of 5 A Day servings: 2.5

Cooking Tip

Use an ice-cream scoop to scoop out the watermelon balls. Remove the seeds, if necessary.

plumberry granita

make ahead

kid-friendly

6	ounces pitted dried plums (about 1 cup)
6	tablespoons hot water
32	ounces white grape juice
1	package (10 ounces) frozen sweetened raspberries, partially thawed
2	tablespoons fresh lemon juice

Cooking Tip

Leftover granita may be refrozen in a covered container. Serve as directed in recipe.

In a blender, combine the dried plums and water; process until the plums are finely chopped. Add the grape juice, raspberries, and lemon juice and puree until smooth. Pour into a shallow metal baking pan. Freeze for 2 hours, stirring every 30 minutes. Freeze for about 2 hours longer, or until completely frozen.

To serve, let the granita stand at room temperature for about 15 minutes, or until slightly softened. Use a metal spoon to scrape across the surface of the granita, transferring the ice shards to chilled dessert dishes or wineglasses without packing them.

Makes 6 servings
Per serving: 225 calories; 1.4 g protein; 57.1 g carbohydrate; 0.4 g fat; 0 mg cholesterol; 6.4 g dietary fiber; 11 mg sodium

Number of 5 A Day servings: 1

spiced peach and dried plum compote

24	ounces white grape juice
3	cinnamon sticks
3 to 4	quarter-size slices peeled fresh ginger (optional)
1	package (12 ounces) dried unpitted plums
1	package (6 ounces) dried peaches or nectarines, cut into strips
3	tablespoons firmly packed brown sugar
2	teaspoons vanilla extract

In a medium saucepan, combine the grape juice, cinnamon sticks, and ginger. Cover and bring to a boil. Reduce the heat and simmer for 5 minutes. Add the dried plums, dried peaches, and brown sugar; simmer for 5 minutes longer, or until the fruit is soft but holds its shape. Remove from the heat and let cool.

Stir in the vanilla; remove the cinnamon sticks and ginger. Transfer to a covered container and refrigerate up to 1 week.

Makes 4 cups (four 1-cup servings)
Per serving: 497 calories; 3.6 g protein; 126.8 g carbohydrate; 1 g fat; 0 mg cholesterol; 16.9 g dietary fiber; 20 mg sodium

Number of 5 A Day servings: 3

quick cook

Brown Sugar Grilled Peaches

When the grill is already fired up, here's a tempting way to enjoy the fresh fruit of summer. Ripe peaches are especially delicious cooked this way, but nectarines, pineapple, and plums also work well. Cut the peaches in half and remove the pits. Brush the cut sides of the fruit with a little melted butter or margarine and sprinkle with brown sugar. Grill over medium heat, cut side up, for several minutes. Turn and grill until the peaches begin to soften but still hold their shape, making sure they do not burn. Serve warm or at room temperature with frozen fat-free vanilla yogurt or with fresh raspberry puree, if desired.

spiced grapes with mango, papaya, and pineapple

make ahead

2	cups seedless grapes
½	cup white wine vinegar
½	cup rum (see Cooking Tip, below)
1	cup sugar
2	tablespoons fresh lime juice
2	tablespoons fine strips fresh ginger
1	teaspoon finely grated lime zest
1	cinnamon stick
3	whole cloves
¼	teaspoon salt
1	mango, peeled and cut into 1-inch cubes
1	papaya, peeled, seeded, and cut into 1-inch cubes
1	cup fresh or canned pineapple chunks

Cooking Tip

½ cup water plus 2 tablespoons rum extract can be substituted for the rum.

Put the grapes into a large bowl. In a small saucepan, combine the vinegar, rum, sugar, lime juice, ginger, lime zest, cinnamon, cloves, and salt. Bring the mixture to a boil; pour over the grapes. Let cool until room temperature.

Add the mango, papaya, and pineapple to the grape mixture. Refrigerate for at least 1 hour, or until thoroughly chilled. Remove the cinnamon stick and cloves. To serve, spoon the fruit into individual dishes.

Makes 6 servings
Per serving: 270 calories; 1.1 g protein; 58.3 g carbohydrate; 0.6 g fat; 0 mg cholesterol; 2.7 g dietary fiber; 104 mg sodium

Number of 5 A Day servings: 1.5

serving suggestion

Serve over flan or baked custard, as a topping for ice cream, or with almond or vanilla cookies.

quick cook

Frozen Grapes

Here's an inventive refresher for a hot summer's day. The only ingredient is seedless grapes, so be sure they are the best you can find. Choose grapes that are plump, fresh-looking, and securely attached to their stems. Avoid any with dry, brittle stems or those that are cracked or leaking moisture. Wash the grapes well and pat completely dry with paper towels. Place small clusters or whole bunches in a baking pan and place in the freezer for several hours, or until just frozen. Transfer to a glass bowl and serve.

chunky northwest pear and fig sauce

2	pounds firm-ripe Anjou or Bosc pears, peeled, cored, and cut into ½-inch pieces (about 4 pounds)
1	package (9 ounces) dried figs, cut into ½-inch pieces
4	ounces orange juice
⅛	teaspoon salt
¼	cup firmly packed brown sugar or honey
	Frozen fat-free vanilla yogurt, for serving (optional)

In a large heavy saucepan, combine the pears, figs, orange juice, and salt. Cover and bring to a boil over high heat. Reduce the heat and simmer, stir occasionally, for 25 to 35 minutes, or until the fruit is soft but still holds its shape. Stir in the brown sugar and optional spices (see Cooking Tip, below), if desired.

Serve warm or at room temperature with frozen vanilla yogurt, if desired. (Can be stored in a covered container in the refrigerator up to 2 weeks.)

Makes 3 cups (six ½-cup servings)
Per serving: 241 calories; 2 g protein; 57 g carbohydrate; 0.5 g fat; 0 mg cholesterol; 9 g dietary fiber; 51 mg sodium

Number of 5 A Day servings: 2

Cooking Tip

You can add other flavorings to this delicious sauce: Along with the brown sugar, stir in ⅛ teaspoon ground cloves and ½ teaspoon ground cinnamon, or for an Asian flavor, add 2 to 3 tablespoons finely chopped candied ginger and ⅛ teaspoon Chinese Five Spice powder.

italian fruit cobbler
with vanilla sauce

Fruit Filling

4	Bartlett pears, peeled, cored, and sliced
3	Granny Smith apples, peeled, cored, and sliced
½	cup dried cranberries
1	tablespoon all-purpose flour
1	tablespoon sugar
2	ounces orange juice

Topping

1	cup all-purpose flour
⅓	cup polenta or yellow cornmeal
¼	cup sugar
1	teaspoon ground cinnamon
4	ounces low-fat cream cheese, at room temperature
2 to 4	tablespoons ice-cold water
	Sugar and ground cinnamon, for sprinkling

Sauce

1	container (8 ounces) fat-free vanilla yogurt
4	ounces fat-free half-and-half

Preheat the oven to 375°F.

To make the filling: In a large bowl, combine the filling ingredients and toss until mixed well. Spoon into an ungreased 9- × 13-inch baking dish.

To make the topping: In a medium bowl, whisk together the flour, polenta, sugar and cinnamon. With a pastry blender or two knives used scissor-fashion, cut in the cream cheese until the mixture resembles baby peas. Sprinkle in the ice water, 1 tablespoon at a time, mixing lightly with a fork after each addition, to form a dry dough that holds together. Carefully spread the dough on top of the fruit and sprinkle with a little sugar and cinnamon.

Bake the cobbler for 40 to 50 minutes, or until the filling is bubbling and the topping is golden.

Meanwhile, in a small bowl, whisk together the sauce ingredients.

To serve, drizzle the sauce in a circle pattern on each plate and top with a portion of the warm cobbler.

Makes 8 servings
Per serving: 264 calories; 5 g protein; 55 g carbohydrate; 3 g fat; 7 mg cholesterol; 3 g dietary fiber; 113 mg sodium

Number of 5 A Day servings: 1

pear-strawberry trifle

make ahead

kid-friendly

2	peeled, cored, and thinly sliced pears
2	cups hulled and coarsely chopped strawberries
2	tablespoons fresh lemon juice
2	tablespoons almond-flavored liqueur or ½ teaspoon almond extract
2	tablespoons orange juice
2	tablespoons honey
½	9-inch angel food cake, cut into 1-inch cubes
3	cups low-fat vanilla or lemon-flavored yogurt
1	cup diced fresh or canned pineapple, drained
	Pear slices and mint sprigs, for garnish

In a medium bowl, combine the pears, strawberries, lemon juice, and almond liqueur and toss until mixed. In a dish, stir together the orange juice and honey.

Assemble the trifle: In a deep 2 to 2½-quart glass bowl, layer one-third of the cake cubes and drizzle with 1 tablespoon of the orange juice mixture. Top with 1 cup of the yogurt, 2 cups of the pear and strawberry mixture, and ½ cup of the pineapple. Repeat the layers once. Cover with the remaining cake, drizzle with the remaining orange juice mixture, and spoon the remaining yogurt over the top. Cover with plastic wrap and refrigerate for at least 1 or up to 4 hours. Garnish the trifle with pear slices and mint sprigs just before serving.

Makes 6 servings
Per serving: 344 calories; 10 g protein; 71.5 g carbohydrate; 2 g fat; 6 mg cholesterol; 3.3 g dietary fiber; 223 mg sodium
Number of 5 A Day servings: 1

quick cook

Instant Fruit Sauce

When unexpected company stops by and you need a little something to dress up plain angel food cake, fresh fruit salad, or sorbet, here is the answer. Take some of your favorite fruit preserves and mix in a blender until chunky smooth. Transfer to a serving bowl and add fresh lemon or lime juice to taste.

pear and cranberry crisp

Topping

1	cup all-purpose flour
⅔	cup firmly packed light brown sugar
½	cup old-fashioned oats
¼	teaspoon salt
8	tablespoons (1 stick) chilled unsalted butter or margarine, cut into pieces

Fruit Filling

7	large slightly under-ripe pears (about 3½ pounds), peeled, cored, and each cut lengthwise into eight slices
1	cup fresh or frozen cranberries
½	cup sugar
2	tablespoons all-purpose flour
½	teaspoon ground cinnamon
¼	teaspoon ground ginger
	Vanilla ice cream (optional)

Place a rack in the middle of the oven and preheat to 350°F. Butter an 8-inch square baking dish with 2-inch sides.

To make the topping: In a medium bowl, mix together the flour, brown sugar, oats, and salt. With a pastry blender or two knives used scissor-fashion, cut in the butter until the mixture resembles coarse meal.

To make the filling: Toss together all the ingredients until well mixed and spoon into the prepared dish. Sprinkle the topping evenly over the filling. Set the dish on a baking sheet to catch any drips.

Bake for about 1 hour, or until the topping is golden and the filling thickens and bubbles. Cool at least 20 minutes. Serve with vanilla ice cream, if desired.

Makes 6 servings
Per serving: 582 calories; 4.8 g protein; 108.7 g carbohydrate; 17.2 g fat; 41 mg cholesterol; 9.1 g dietary fiber; 110 mg sodium

Number of 5 A Day servings: 1.5

quick cook

Roasted Pears with Honey

Roasting pears can improve their flavor. Peel the pears and remove the cores. Make sure the bottom of each pear is flat. Brush the pears with melted butter and roll in sugar. Stand them vertically in a shallow baking pan and pour about ¾ cup water into the pan. Roast the pears at 425°F, brushing them occasionally with the liquid in the bottom of the pan, until they are tender, about 40 minutes. Serve warm or at room temperature with honey drizzled over them.

plum-raspberry dessert soup

make ahead

1½	pounds plums (about 8 medium), sliced
1	cup fresh or frozen raspberries
1½	cups dry red wine
3	cinnamon sticks
½	cup water
1	tablespoon cornstarch
2 to 3	tablespoons sugar
	Frozen low-fat vanilla yogurt, for serving (optional)
	Mint sprigs, for garnish

In a large saucepan, combine the plums, raspberries, wine, and cinnamon sticks. Bring to a boil over medium-high heat. Reduce the heat and simmer for 15 minutes, or until the fruit is very soft. In a cup, blend the water and cornstarch until smooth. Whisk into the soup; cook, stirring until the soup thickens and boils. Remove from the heat and add sugar to taste; remove the cinnamon sticks. Cool the soup.

In a blender, puree the soup until smooth. Pour into a covered container and refrigerate until well chilled. (Can be refrigerated up to 2 days.)

To serve, ladle the soup into shallow bowls. Drop a small scoop of frozen yogurt into the center of each serving, if desired. Garnish with mint sprigs.

Makes 6 servings.
Per serving: 143 calories; 9.3 g protein; 23 g carbohydrate; 1.5 g fat; 4 mg cholesterol; 3 g dietary fiber; 10 mg sodium

Number of 5 A Day servings: 1

no-guilt watermelon "cake"

1   uniformly shaped seedless
    watermelon (7 to 9 inches in
    diameter)

½   container (8 ounces) frozen
    nondairy whipped topping,
    thawed

1   container (8 ounces) fat-free
    lemon yogurt
    Strawberries, kiwifruit, grapes,
    and blueberries, for decoration

Cut a 3-inch-thick cross-section slice from the middle of the watermelon. With a serrated knife, and using a sawing motion, cut all around the slice to separate the white portion of the rind from the red flesh. Lift up the ring of rind and remove. Pat the watermelon dry with paper towels and set on a flat serving plate.

In a small bowl, fold together the whipped topping and yogurt. With a narrow metal spatula, frost the top and side of the watermelon cake with the yogurt mixture. Decorate with fresh fruit. Refrigerate until ready to serve. (Can be refrigerated for several hours or up to overnight.) Cut into wedges and serve.

Makes 6 servings
Per serving without fruit garnish: 171 calories; 2.9 g protein; 44.2 g carbohydrate; 0 g fat; 0.6 mg cholesterol; 1.9 g dietary fiber; 56 mg sodium

Number of 5 A Day servings: 1

watermelon
with fresh raspberry sauce

kid-friendly

⅓	cup raspberry vinegar
2	tablespoons sugar
1	cup raspberries (about ½ pint)
4	watermelon wedges with their rind, chilled
	Mint sprigs, for garnish

In a small saucepan, combine the vinegar and sugar and bring to a boil over medium heat, stirring until the sugar dissolves. Remove from the heat and stir in the raspberries. Place the watermelon wedges on plates and spoon the raspberry mixture over. Garnish with mint sprigs and serve.

Makes 4 servings
Per serving: 195 calories, 3 g protein; 45 g carbohydrate; 2 g fat; 0 mg cholesterol; 2 g dietary fiber; 10 mg sodium

Number of 5 A Day servings: 1.5

credits

The following members of the Produce for Better Health Foundation contributed recipes to the book. Log on to their Web sites (included below) for more recipes.

Alaska Department of Health
3601 C Street
Suite 934
P.O. Box 240249
Anchorage, AK 99524
(907) 269-3463
www.hss.state.ak.us

Recipes: Fisherman's Salmon with Rice and Tomatoes; Governor's Black Bean Soup; Potato–Double Cheese Gratin; Warm Blueberry Cobbler

Almond Board of California
1150 Ninth Street
Suite 1500
Modesto, California 95354
(209) 549-8262
www.almondsarein.com

Recipes: Baked Almond Sole with Warm Wild Rice Salad (photo, p. 194); Mesclun Salad with Spicy Almonds and Turkey; Smoked Trout Salad with Oranges and Almonds; Dried Fruit and Almond Granola with Yogurt and Banana (photo, p. 59 and back cover)

California Asparagus Commission
4565 Quarie Lakes Drive

Suite A-1
Stockton, CA 95207
(209) 474-7581
www.calasparagus.com

Recipes: Asparagus and Blood Orange Salad; Asparagus Tapas with Red Pepper Sauce; Baked Asparagus with Parmesan Cheese; Chicken Oriental; Springtime Scallop and Asparagus Stir-Fry; Steamed Salmon with Walnut Vinaigrette

California Avocado Commission
1251 E. Dyer Road #210
Santa Ana, CA 90254
(714) 558-6761
www.avocado.org

Recipes: Avocado and Smoked Turkey Salad in Bread Baskets (photo, p. 188); California Avocado Tacos; California Fruit Salad; Fettuccine with Avocado; Pasta Salad Niçoise with Avocado

California Dried Plum Board
3841 North Freeway Blvd.
P.O. Box 348180
Sacramento, CA 95834
(916) 565-6232
www.prunes.org

Recipes: Apple–Dried Plum Chutney; Citrus Slaw (photo, p. 72); East Meets West Stir-Fry; Plumberry Granita

California Fig Advisory Board
3425 North 1st Street, Suite 109
Fresno, California 93726
(800) 588-2344
www.californiafigs.com

Recipes: Dried Fig and Fruit Salsa; Fig, Apple, and Chicken Stir-Fry

California Kiwifruit Commission
9845 Horn Road, Suite 160
Sacramento, CA 95827
(916) 362-7490
www.kiwifruit.org

Recipes: California Chicken and Kiwifruit Salad; Kiwifruit-Mango Salsa

California Pear Advisory Board
1521 I Street
Sacramento, CA 95814
(916) 441-0432
www.calpear.com

Recipes: Bartlett Pear and Mango Salsa (photo, p. 66); Confetti Pear and Spinach Salad (photo, p. 72); Pear and Cranberry Crisp (photo, p. 202)

California Strawberry Commission
1050 Battery Street
San Francisco, CA 94111
(831) 724-1301
www.calstrawberry.com

Recipes: After-School Strawberry Shake (photo, p. 61); Strawberry and Turkey Spa Salad; Strawberry Chef's Salad (photo, p. 189); Strawberry Fruit Salad with Three

Dressings (photo, p. 69); Strawberry Sangria Ice (photo, p. 63)

California Table Grape Commission
392 W. Fallbrook Avenue, Suite 101
Fresno, CA 93711
(559) 447-8350
www.tablegrape.com

Recipes: Balsamic Chicken Salad (photo, p. 187 and back cover); Curried Grape Salsa (photo, p. 65); Grilled Grapes (photo, p. 197); Spiced Grapes with Mango, Papaya, and Pineapple (photo, p. 201); Wild Grape Slush (photo, p. 62)

California Tree Fruit Agreement
975 I Street
Reedley, CA 93654
(559) 638-8260
www.caltreefruit.com

Recipes: Chilled Nectarine Soup; Confetti Plum-Pasta Salad; Fruited Chicken Paprika; Nectarines with Sea Scallops; Plum-Raspberry Dessert Soup; Warm Plum and Smoked Chicken Salad

D'Arrigo Brothers Company
(Andy Boy® Vegetables)
383 West Market Street
Salinas, CA 93901
(831) 424-3955
www.andyboy.com

Recipes: Penne Salad with Broccoli Rabe (photo, p. 74)

Dean Foods/Marie's
10255 W. Higgins Road, Suite 500
Rosemont, IL 60018
(847) 233-5448
www.deanfoods.com

Recipes: Honey-Dijon Chicken with Peach-Cilantro Salsa; Roasted Chicken Salad with Raspberry Vinaigrette (photo, p. 189)

Del Monte Fresh Produce/
Orchard Select
800 Douglas Entrance
North Tower 11th Floor
Coral Gables, FL 33134
(305) 520-8400
www.freshdelmonte.com

Recipes: Cold Honeydew-Lime Soup; Fruit Basket Waffles; Greens with Pineapple, Apple, and Feta; Honey Dijon and Pear Salad; Tropical Fruit Ambrosia

Dole Food Company
One Dole Drive
Westlake Village, CA 91362
(818) 879-6600
www.dole.com

Recipes: Catfish with Tropical Fruit Salsa (photo, p. 192); Cool Summer Gazpacho Salad (photo, p. 74); Garden-Style Risotto (photo, p. 198); Island Shake; Mediterranean Pasta Salad; Pork Tenderloin with Orange-Basil Sauce (photo, p. 190); Tropical Breakfast Parfait

Florida Department of Citrus
P.O. Box 148
1115 East Memorial Boulevard
Lakeland, FL 33802
(863) 499-2500
www.floridajuice.com

Recipes: Cinnamon Oatmeal with Fruit and Nuts; Citrus Salad with Raspberry-Vanilla Sauce; Grapefruit Fizz; Orange Chicken with Citrus Salsa; Skillet Sweet Potatoes; Spinach-Citrus Salad

Florida Tomato Committee
P.O. Box 140635
4401 E. Colonial Drive
Orlando, FL 32814
(407) 894-3071
www.floridatomatoes.org

Recipes: Blackened Tomato Soup; Chunky Fresh Tomato Salsa; Cioppino; Green Beans with Tomato, Basil, and Goat Cheese; Grilled Southwestern Shrimp (photo, p. 193); Pasta with Shrimp, Tomatoes, and Feta (photo, p. 194); Sole with Fresh Tomatoes and Olives; Spaghetti Squash with Chunky Tomato-Garlic Sauce (photo, p. 199); Tomato, Garlic, and Pesto Omelet (photo, p. 59)

Grimmway Farms
P.O. Box 87498
Bakersfield, CA 93380
(661) 845-5229
www.grimmway.com

Recipes: Lemon Carrots; Roasted Carrots

Louisiana Sweet Potato
Commission
P.O. Box 2550
Baton Rouge, LA 70821
(225) 922-1277
www.sweetpotatoes.org

Recipes: Southwestern Pork Stew; Sweet Potato–Bean Burritos; Sweet Potato–Cranberry Galette; Sweet Potato Pancakes with Apple-Walnut Topping; Sweet Potato, Pineapple, and Pecan Salad; Twice-Baked Yams; Two-Potato Bisque

Michigan Apple Committee
12800 Escanaba Drive, Suite B
DeWitt, MI 48820

(800) 456-2753

www.michiganapples.com

Recipes: Appleade; Baked Apple Fritters

Mott's
6 High Ridge Park
Stamford, CT 06905
(203) 968-7757
www.motts.com

Recipes: Applesauce with Crunchy Topping; Banana–Apple Sherbet

The Mushroom Council
11875 Dublin Blvd.
Suite D 262
Dublin, CA 94568
(925) 556-5970
www.mushroomcouncil.com

Recipes: Grilled Turkey-Mushroom Burgers with Chutney Sauce; Moroccan Couscous with Mushrooms; Polenta, Spinach, and Mushroom Lasagna; Red Snapper, Mushroom, and Black Olive Packets; Thai-Style Marinated Mushrooms (photo, p. 64); Wilted Spinach Salad

National Cancer Institute
Office of Communications and
Health Promotion
Building 31, Room 10A03
MSC 2580
Bethesda, MD 20892
(301) 435-3848
www.nci.nih.gov

Recipes: Bowties with Tomato-Pepper Sauce; Broccoli and Green Beans with Green Sauce; Cherokee Corn and Beans with Acorn Squash; Curried Rice with Roasted Carrots and Apricots;

Italian Fruit Cobbler with Vanilla Sauce; Mixed Greens with Strawberries and Orange; South of the Border Squash Soup (photo, p. 68); Vietnamese Cabbage Salad (photo, p. 73)

National Onion
Association
822 7th Street, Suite 510
Greeley, CO 80631
(970) 353-5895
www.onions-usa.org

Recipes: Caramelized Onions (photo, p. 196); Creamy Onion Dip (photo, p. 64); Crispy Beer-Batter Onion Rings

National Watermelon Board
3660 Maguire Blvd., Suite 212
P.O. Box 140065
Orlando, FL 32814
(407) 895-5100
www.watermelon.org

Recipes: Caribbean Salsa (photo, p. 67); No-Guilt Watermelon "Cake" (photo, p. 202); Watermelon-Blueberry Banana Split (photo, p. 201); Watermelon Gazpacho; Watermelon-Strawberry Shake (photo, p. 61); Watermelon with Fresh Raspberry Sauce

North American Blueberry Council
4995 Golden Foothill Parkway
Suite #2
El Dorado Hills, CA 95762
(916) 933-9399
www.blueberry.org

Recipes: Blueberry Fruit Shake; Blueberry-Pineapple Parfaits

Northwest Cherry Growers
105 S. 18th Street
Yakima, WA 98901
(509) 453-4837
www.nwcherries.org

Recipes: Cherry-Couscous Salad; Grilled Cherry-Vegetable Kebabs (photo, p. 195); Northwest Cherry and Tropical Fruit Salad; Root 'N' Cherry Salad (photo, p. 70); Spicy Cherry Chutney

Ocean Mist Farms
10855 Cara Mia Parkway
Castroville, CA 95012
(831) 633-2144
www.oceanmist.com

Recipes: Artichokes Stuffed with Oriental Noodle Salad (photo, p. 195)

The Peanut Institute
c/o PMK Associates
2416 13th Court North
Arlington, VA 22201
(703) 841-1600
www.peanut-institute.org

Recipes: Peanut Hummus and Fresh Veggies

Pear Bureau Northwest
4382 SE International Way, Suite A
Milwaukee, OR 97222
(503) 652-9720
www.nwpear.com

Recipes: Northwest Pear Slush; Pear-Strawberry Trifle (photo, p. 200); Sweet Potato–Pear Soup

Sunkist Growers
14130 Riverside Drive
Sherman Oaks, CA 91423
(818) 379-7467
www.sunkist.com

Recipes: Chicken and Grapefruit Stir-Fry (photo, p. 190); Confetti Fruit Salad (photo, p. 71); Lemony Bean Salad; Orange-Sesame Couscous (photo, p. 199); Scandinavian Baked Halibut Dinner (photo, p. 193); Tangy Fresh Orangeade (photo, p. 63)

Sunsweet Growers
9010 N. Walton Avenue
Yuba City, CA 95993
(800) 417-2253
www.sunsweet.com

Recipes: Mexican Steak and Fruit Skewers (photo, p. 191); Roasted Vegetables and Fruit with Citrus-Thyme Vinaigrette (photo, p. 196); Sesame Chicken Kebabs; Spiced Peach and Dried Plum Compote; Spring Salad with Dried Plums and Lemon Vinaigrette; Tropical Fruit with Lime Dressing

TexaSweet Citrus Marketing, Inc.
901 Business Park Drive, Suite 100
Mission, TX 78572
(956) 580-8004
www.texasweet.com

Recipes: Rio Breakfast Shake; Rio Grande Spinach Salad; Texas Breakfast Parfait (photo, p. 60); Texas-Style Citrus Salsa (photo, p. 67)

Tree Top, Inc.
220 E. 2nd Avenue
Selah, WA 98942
(509) 698-1454
www.treetop.com

Recipes: Hot Spiced Cider

Valley Fig Growers
P.O. Box 1987
Fresno, CA 93718
(559) 237-3893
www.valleyfig.com

Recipes: Chunky Northwest Pear and Fig Sauce; Pork Medallions with Honey-Glazed Fruit

Washington Apple Commission
P.O. Box 18
2900 Euclid Avenue
Wenatchee, WA 98807
(509) 663-9600
www.bestapples.com

Recipes: Apple-Beet Salad; Apple-Fennel Soup; Crunchy Apple-Walnut Salad (photo, p. 70)

Olween Woodier
17642 Camby Road
Leesburg, VA 20175
(703) 771-3056

Recipes: Asian Apple-Chicken Salad; Triple Fruit Smoothie

index

Underscored page references indicate boxed text. **Boldface** references indicate photographs.

d

g

Garlic
  health benefits of, 7
  peeling, 146
  roasting, 94
  Spaghetti Squash with Chunky
    Tomato-Garlic Sauce, **198**,
    205
  Spicy Broccoli with Garlic and
    Parmesan, 165
  storing, 182
  Tomato, Garlic, and Pesto
    Omelet, 44, **59**
  uses for, 19
  White Bean and Garlic Spread,
    81
Ginger
  Strawberry-Ginger Dressing,
    68, 111
Glazes
  Confectioners' Sugar Glaze, 214
Goat cheese
  Green Beans with Tomato,
    Basil, and Goat Cheese, 177
Granita
  Plumberry Granita, 218
  refreezing, 218
Granola
  Blueberry-Pineapple Parfaits, 38
  Dried Fruit and Almond
    Granola with Yogurt and
    Banana, 39, **59**
  Texas Breakfast Parfait, 41, **60**
Grape(s)
  Avocado and Smoked Turkey
    Salad in Bread Baskets, 134,
    188
  Balsamic Chicken Salad, 129
  Blueberry Fruit Shake, 50
  Curried Grape Salsa, **65**, 79
  Frozen Grapes, 220
  Fruit Basket Waffles, 42
  Grilled Grapes, 182, **197**
  health benefits of, 7, 12
  Spiced Grapes with Mango,
    Papaya, and Pineapple,
    201, 220

Strawberry and Turkey Spa
  Salad, 137
Tropical Fruit with Lime
  Dressing, 108
Wild Grape Slush, 46, **62**
Grapefruit
  California Fruit Salad, 109
  Chicken and Grapefruit Stir-
    Fry, 146, **190**
  Citrus Salad with Raspberry-
    Vanilla Sauce, 104
  health benefits of, 7
  Orange Chicken with Citrus
    Salsa, 151
  Rio Breakfast Shake, 51
  Rio Grande Spinach Salad,
    122
  storing, 20
  Strawberry Chef's Salad, 136,
    189
  Strawberry Fruit Salad with
    Three Dressings, **68**, 111
  Texas Breakfast Parfait, 41,
    60
  Texas-Style Citrus Salsa, **67**, 78
Grapefruit juice
  Cinnamon Oatmeal with Fruit
    and Nuts, 40
  Grapefruit Fizz, 46
Grape juice
  Plumberry Granita, 218
  Spiced Peach and Dried Plum
    Compote, 219
Green beans
  Broccoli and Green Beans
    with Green Sauce, 176
  Green Beans with Tomato,
    Basil, and Goat Cheese, 177
  Shrimp and Vegetable Egg
    Rolls, 76
  storing, 182
Green olives
  Sole with Fresh Tomatoes and
    Olives, 171
Green peppers. *See* Bell peppers
Green vegetables. *See* Leafy
  green vegetables; *and
  specific types*
Gremolata, 175

Grilled dishes
  Brown Sugar Grilled Peaches,
    219
  Grilled Grapes, 182, **197**
  Grilled Southwestern Shrimp,
    167, **193**
  Grilled Turkey-Mushroom
    Burgers with Chutney
    Sauce, 153

h

Haddock
  Cioppino, 161
Halibut
  Scandinavian Baked Halibut
    Dinner, 162, **193**
Ham
  Baked Manicotti with
    Asparagus, 138
  Pasta with Cherry Tomatoes
    and Parsley, 140
Hands
  cleaning up after snacks, 10
  washing, 51
Health benefits of 5 A Day plan,
  5–10
Heart disease, prevention of, 5–6,
  7, 12
Herbs
  fresh, storing, 167
  uses for, 19
High blood pressure, control of,
  6, 8
Homocysteine, lowering levels
  of, 6
Honey
  Orange-Honey Dressing,
    125
  Pork Medallions with Honey-
    Glazed Fruit, 155
  Roasted Pears with Honey,
    224
Honeydew melon
  Blueberry Fruit Shake, 50
  Cold Honeydew-Lime Soup,
    90

Conversion Chart

These equivalents have been slightly rounded to make measuring easier.

Volume Measurements

U.S.	Imperial	Metric
¼ tsp	–	1 ml
½ tsp	–	2 ml
1 tsp	–	5 ml
1 Tbsp	–	15 ml
2 Tbsp (1 oz)	1 fl oz	30 ml
¼ cup (2 oz)	2 fl oz	60 ml
⅓ cup (3 oz)	3 fl oz	80 ml
½ cup (4 oz)	4 fl oz	120 ml
⅔ cup (5 oz)	5 fl oz	160 ml
¾ cup (6 oz)	6 fl oz	180 ml
1 cup (8 oz)	8 fl oz	240 ml

Weight Measurements

U.S.	Metric
1 oz	30 g
2 oz	60 g
4 oz (¼ lb)	115 g
5 oz (⅓ lb)	145 g
6 oz	170 g
7 oz	200 g
8 oz (½ lb)	230 g
10 oz	285 g
12 oz (¾ lb)	340 g
14 oz	400 g
16 oz (1 lb)	455 g
2.2 lb	1 kg

Length Measurements

U.S.	Metric
¼"	0.6 cm
½"	1.25 cm
1"	2.5 cm
2"	5 cm
4"	11 cm
6"	15 cm
8"	20 cm
10"	25 cm
12" (1')	30 cm

Pan Sizes

U.S.	Metric
8" cake pan	20 × 4 cm sandwich or cake tin
9" cake pan	23 × 3.5 cm sandwich or cake tin
11" × 7" baking pan	28 × 18 cm baking tin
13" × 9" baking pan	32.5 × 23 cm baking tin
15" × 10" baking pan	38 × 25.5 cm baking tin (Swiss roll tin)
1½ qt baking dish	1.5 liter baking dish
2 qt baking dish	2 liter baking dish
2 qt rectangular baking dish	30 × 19 cm baking dish
9" pie plate	22 × 4 or 23 × 4 cm pie plate
7" or 8" springform pan	18 or 20 cm springform or loose-bottom cake tin
9" × 5" loaf pan	23 × 13 cm or 2 lb narrow loaf tin or pâté tin

Temperatures

Fahrenheit	Centigrade	Gas
140°	60°	–
160°	70°	–
180°	80°	–
225°	105°	¼
250°	120°	½
275°	135°	1
300°	150°	2
325°	160°	3
350°	180°	4
375°	190°	5
400°	200°	6
425°	220°	7
450°	230°	8
475°	245°	9
500°	260°	–